Quick Study

Science

PEARSON

Scott Foresman

Editorial Offices: Glenview, Illinois • Parsippany, New Jersey • New York, New York
Sales Offices: Needham, Massachusetts • Duluth, Georgia • Glenview, Illinois
Coppell, Texas • Ontario, California • Mesa, Arizona

www.sfsuccessnet.com

Series Authors

Dr. Timothy Cooney
Professor of Earth Science and Science Education
University of Northern Iowa (UNI)
Cedar Falls, Iowa

Dr. James Flood
Distinguished Professor of Literacy and Language
School of Teacher Education
San Diego State University
San Diego, California

Barbara Foots
Science Education Consultant
Houston, Texas

Dr. M. Jenice Goldston
Associate Professor of Science Education
Department of Elementary Education Programs
University of Alabama
Tuscaloosa, Alabama

Dr. Shirley Gholston Key
Associate Professor of Science Education
Instruction and Curriculum Leadership Department
College of Education
University of Memphis
Memphis, Tennessee

Dr. Diane Lapp
Distinguished Professor of Reading and Language Arts in Teacher Education
San Diego State University
San Diego, California

Sheryl Alicia Mercier, Ma.Ed.
Classroom Teacher
Dunlap Elementary School
Dunlap, California

Dr. Karen Ostlund
Director
UTeach | Dell Center for New Teacher Success
The University of Texas at Austin
Austin, Texas

Dr. Nancy Romance
Professor of Science Education & Principal Investigator
NSF/IERI Science IDEAS Project
Charles E. Schmidt College of Science
Florida Atlantic University
Boca Raton, Florida

Dr. William Tate
Chair and Professor of Education and Applied Statistics
Department of Education
Washington University
St Louis, Missouri

Dr. Kathryn C. Thornton
Professor
School of Engineering and Applied Science
University of Virginia
Charlottesville, Virginia

Dr. Leon Ukens
Professor or Science Education
Department of Physics, Astronomy, and Geosciences
Towson University
Towson, Maryland

Steve Weinberg
Consultant
Connecticut Center for Advanced Technology
East Hartford, Connecticut

Dr. Jim Cummins
Professor
Modern Language Center & Curriculum Department
Ontario Institute for Studies in Education
Toronto, Canada

Consulting Author

Dr. Michael P. Klentschy
Superintendent
El Centro Elementary School District
El Centro, California

ISBN: 0-328-14576-9

Unit A
Life Science

Unit B
Earth Science

Unit C
Physical Science

Unit D
Space and Technology

Lesson 1: What are the building blocks of life?

Vocabulary

cell the building block of life

nucleus the control center of a cell

cytoplasm a gel-like liquid inside the cell membrane that contains the things that the cell needs to carry out life processes

chloroplast a special part of a plant that traps the energy in sunlight for making food

What Cells Are

A **cell** is the smallest part of a living thing. A cell can only come from other living cells.

All living things are made of cells. Some living things are made of just one cell. Most living things have many cells. For example, a cat has muscles, blood, and fur. Each of these parts is made of thousands of cells.

Different cells have different jobs. Some cells help an animal get energy. Other cells help it move or stay healthy.

Most cells are very small. They are hard to see. Scientists use microscopes to study cells. A microscope is a tool. It makes things look larger than they are.

The Parts of a Cell

Bugs, birds, and animals look different. But their cells have some of the same parts. These parts have special jobs. The **nucleus** tells the cell what to do. The cell membrane lets things move in and out of the cell. Cells also have **cytoplasm.** It has what cells need in order to live.

Cells Working Together

A plant or animal can have many cells. Different kinds of cells do different kinds of work. Groups of the same cells make up tissues. For example, groups of cardiac muscle cells make up cardiac muscle tissue.

Each kind of tissue does something different. A group of tissues that work together to do a special job makes an organ. For example, cardiac muscle tissue makes up most of the heart. The heart is an organ.

A group of organs that work together make up an organ system. The heart, blood, and blood vessels make up the circulatory system. This system pumps blood around the body. A living thing is made of all these parts: the tissues, organs, and organ systems.

Like animal cells, plant cells have a cell membrane, cytoplasm, and a nucleus. Unlike animal cells, plant cells need special parts to make their own food. These parts are called chloroplasts. They trap the energy in sunlight. Plants need this energy to make food.

Plants also have a cell wall. The cell wall is outside of the cell membrane. It helps support each part of the plant.

Lesson 1 Checkpoint

1. Why are cells considered the building blocks of living things?

_____

_____

2. Describe the difference between a cell, a tissue, and an organ.

_____

_____

3. Can a single-celled organism contain tissue? Explain.

_____

_____

4. **Compare and Contrast** Make a graphic organizer to compare and contrast animal and plant cells.

_____

_____

_____

_____

Lesson 2: How are living things grouped?

Vocabulary

genus a group of closely related living things

species a group of similar organisms that can mate and produce offspring

Classification Systems

The world has over a million kinds of organisms. Scientists use a classification system to identify, compare, and study them. This system sorts organisms into different groups. All organisms in a group are the same in some way. Are a dandelion and a mushroom in the same group? Scientists decide by asking questions about their characteristics:

How many cells does it have? Some organisms have only one cell. But a dandelion has plant organs made of many cells. A mushroom also has more than one cell.

Where does it live? Dandelions and mushrooms live on land. Mushrooms can also grow on dead trees.

How does it get food? A dandelion makes its own food. A mushroom gets its food from other living or dead things.

Both the dandelion and mushroom have more than one cell. They live on land. The dandelion makes its own food; the mushroom does not. They are in different groups.

Kingdoms

A kingdom is the largest classification group. Many scientists classify organisms into six kingdoms. Scientists look at how many cells and cell parts an organism has. They also look at where an organism lives and how it gets food. All animals belong to one kingdom. All plants belong to another kingdom.

Kingdoms of Living Things

These are the six kingdoms:

Ancient bacteria have only one cell. They do not have a separate nucleus. They live on land or in water. They also make their own food.

True bacteria also have one cell with no separate nucleus. They live on land or in water. Some make their own food.

Protists have a nucleus and other cell parts. They live in water and damp places. Some make their own food. Algae are protists.

Fungi are mostly made of many cells. Each cell has a nucleus and other cell parts. Fungi live on land. They get food from other living or nonliving things. Mushrooms are fungi.

Plants are made of many cells. Each cell has a nucleus and a cell wall. Most plants live on land. They use the sun's energy to make their own food.

Animals are made of many cells. They live on land or in water. Animals eat plants or other animals.

Getting More Specific

Scientists divide kingdoms into smaller and smaller groups. The first part of an organism's scientific name is its **genus.** Animals that are closely related are in the same group, called a genus. For example, lions and house cats are in the genus *Felis.* The second part of an organism's scientific name is its **species.** A species is a group of similar organisms that can produce offspring. The species name describes something about the organism, like its color.

Lesson 2 Checkpoint

1. Why is a classification system important to scientists?

_____

_____

2. What are some of the characteristics scientists use to classify organisms?

_____

_____

3. In what kingdoms would you expect to find living things that can make their own food?

_____

_____

Lesson 3: How are plants classified?

How Plants Transport Water and Nutrients

One way biologists classify plants is by how they move food and water. For example, bamboo is a very tall plant. How do the cells at the top of this plant get food and water from the soil? Bamboo has tissues that make a system of tubes. Food and water move up and down these tubes. The tubes feed all the plant's organs—its leaves, stems, and roots. Plants that move food and water through tubes are called vascular plants. Grass, celery, and trees are all vascular.

Vascular tissue also supports a plant's stem and leaves. This helps vascular plants to grow larger.

More Down-to-Earth Plants

Plants that do not move food and water through tubes are called nonvascular plants. These plants don't have real roots, stems, or leaves. They can only pass food and water from one cell to another. The food and water do not travel very far or quickly. Nonvascular plants are usually small. They can grow so close together that they look like one plant. Most live in moist places.

Mosses are nonvascular plants. They look like a green mat. They can live in cold places. Mosses do not have true stems or leaves. They can make their own food.

Hornworts are another kind of nonvascular plant. Like mosses, they don't have true stems or leaves. They live in warm places.

The liverwort is a nonvascular plant. It grows on rocks or near streams.

How Plants Make New Plants

Another way biologists classify plants is by how they make new plants. Plants that have flowers make seeds. A seed has many cells. A young plant sits inside the seed. The seed protects this plant. A cactus, fruit tree, and a poppy are all flowering plants.

Some plants make seeds but do not have flowers. These plants are called conifers. Conifers grow cones that have seeds in them. Most conifers are evergreen plants, like pine trees. They keep their leaves, or needles, all year long.

Plants like ferns and mosses do not make seeds. They make tiny cells that can grow into new plants. The cells are called spores. They are different sizes and shapes. Each spore is a made of one cell that has a cell wall. A spore gets its food in wet and shady places. Ferns produce spore sacs on the underside of its leaves. These sacs look like brown dots. In mosses, spores are in cases. Each spore case has hundreds of spores.

Both seeds and spores can grow into new plants. Both seeds and spores can be many different sizes and shapes. But a seed has many cells, while a spore is one cell. A spore needs to get nutrients to grow. A seed has a young plant and stored food inside its cover.

© Pearson Education, Inc. 4

Quick Study

Lesson 3 Checkpoint

1. What are some examples of vascular plants?

_____

_____

2. What are conifers?

_____

_____

3. Name one way of classifying plants into two groups.

_____

_____

4. **Compare and Contrast** How are seeds and spores alike? How are they different?

_____

_____

Lesson 4: How are animals classified?

Vocabulary

vertebrates animals that have a backbone

invertebrates animals that do not have a backbone

Animals with Backbones

Scientists divide the animal kingdom into two groups. All the animals in one group have backbones. They are called **vertebrates.** There are five groups of vertebrates: fishes, amphibians, birds, mammals, and reptiles.

Most *fish* are covered with scales. They live in water and breathe with gills. Most fish are also cold-blooded. This means that their body temperature changes as their environment changes. Fish lay eggs.

Amphibians have wet skin. They can live on land and in the water. Amphibians breathe with lungs, gills, or both. They are cold-blooded. Most amphibians lay eggs.

Birds are covered with feathers. They usually live on land. Birds breathe with lungs. They are warm-blooded. This means their body temperature usually stays the same. Birds also lay eggs.

All *mammals* have hair or fur. Most live on land, but some live in water. They breathe with lungs. Mammals are warm-blooded. Most mammals give live birth.

Reptiles have dry skin and are covered with scales or plates. Most reptiles live on land. Some live in water. They breathe with lungs. Reptiles are cold-blooded. They usually lay eggs instead of giving live birth. Alligators, crocodiles, snakes, and turtles are reptiles.

Life Cycle of a Reptile

The Burmese python is a long, thick snake. It can grow up to 6 meters (about 20 feet) and weigh up to 91 kilograms (about 200 pounds). It squeezes its prey and swallows it whole.

A python's life begins as an egg. After mating, a mother python can lay as many as 100 eggs. She wraps herself around the eggs for 6 to 8 weeks to keep them warm. When the eggs hatch, they are about 51 centimeters (20 inches) long and weigh about 113 grams (4 ounces). The pythons grow to be adults and reproduce. They can live up to 25 years.

Invertebrates

Most animals are **invertebrates.** They do not have a backbone. Jellyfish, worms, insects, spiders, and lobsters are invertebrates. Snails and clams have soft bodies inside hard shells. Jellyfish and worms do not have shells.

Arthropods are the largest group of invertebrates. They have jointed legs. Their bodies have a hard outer skin called an exoskeleton. It protects the arthropod. Insects, spiders, crabs, and shrimp are arthropods.

Mollusks are the second largest group of invertebrates. Clams, octopuses, snails, sea slugs, and squids are mollusks. Most live in water, but some live on land in damp places.

What Is the Life Cycle of a Mollusk?

A snail is a mollusk. Most snails have a shell. They move with a foot. It releases a slimy liquid that makes it easier for the snail to move. Snails usually lay eggs during warm, damp weather.

A brown garden snail's life cycle begins as an egg. A mother snail can lay up to 85 eggs at one time. They hatch in 2 to 4 weeks. Baby snails must find their own food. They become adults in about 2 years. The snail's shell grows as the snail grows. Snails can live up to 10 years.

© Pearson Education, Inc. 4

Lesson 4 Checkpoint

1. What are the five divisions of vertebrates?

_____

_____

2. What happens to a Burmese python egg after the mother has kept it warm for six to eight weeks?

_____

_____

3. Name some animals that are classified as arthropods.

_____

_____

4. Are there more vertebrates or invertebrates on Earth?

_____

_____

5. Name the largest group of invertebrates.

_____

_____

6. **Compare and Contrast** the life cycles of Burmese pythons and brown garden snails.

_____

_____

_____

Lesson 5: How do animals adapt?

How Animals Get What They Need

Young animals get traits from their parents. A trait is a physical feature, such as eye color. Animals are also born knowing behaviors that help them survive. They learn other behaviors.

An adaptation is a physical feature or behavior. It helps animals move, get food, protect themselves, or reproduce. Birds and mammals have adaptations. The shape of a bird's beak helps it get food. Polar bears have fur coats that keep them warm in cold weather. Their sharp claws help them catch and eat food.

Every animal needs food, water, oxygen, and shelter. Sometimes there are not enough of these resources for each animal. Animals with better adaptations have a better chance of getting what they need. They have a better chance of survival.

Adaptations That Protect Animals

Some animals have adaptations to keep them from being eaten by predators. The color, shape, or patterns of animals can help them blend into their environment. For example, Mandarin fish live in bright coral reefs. The fish blend into this environment because they are very colorful. This adaptation makes it hard for other animals to see the Mandarin fish. Animals also use stingers, claws, or smells to protect themselves. Some frogs and toads can even squirt poison.

Animal Instincts

Instincts are behaviors that organisms inherit from their parents. Animals have instincts to help them live. For example, ducklings are born with the instinct to follow their mother. This helps them get protection and food.

Migration

In winter, plants stop growing. Insects die or bury themselves. This means that many animals cannot find enough food. Some of these animals migrate. Migration is traveling to find food or a place to reproduce. Canada geese live in Canada and the northern United States during spring and summer. In winter, they migrate south to find a warmer climate and food.

There are many barriers to migration. Some barriers are man-made, like roads or parking lots. Barriers make it hard or impossible for animals to migrate. For example, the red land crab migrates from the rain forest to the ocean. Sometimes, they must travel over busy roads or across parking lots. Cars or trucks hit some of these crabs.

Other barriers are natural. White storks must cross the Mediterranean Sea to get to their winter homes in Africa.

Migration is a natural behavior for organisms. They do not have to learn it.

Hibernation and Inactivity

During hibernation, animals slow down their body functions. Some mammals, reptiles, and amphibians hibernate during the winter. They move only once in a while to warm themselves or to eat. Some organisms stay still. They get their energy from stored body fat. Hibernation helps animals to survive cold weather.

How Animals Learn

Some behaviors are partly instinct and partly learned. Young animals learn by practicing new behaviors. They see which behaviors help them and which do not. For example, a white-crowned sparrow is born knowing what its song sounds like. This is instinct. But it does not know how to sing the song. The sparrow learns how to sing the song from its parents.

Lesson 5 Checkpoint

1. What is an adaptation?

_____

_____

2. Name some adaptations that animals use to avoid predators.

_____

_____

3. How do the instincts of migration and hibernation help animals to survive?

_____

_____

4. Explain the difference between instinct and learned behavior.

_____

_____

5. How do the adaptation of body color and patterns help the Mandarin fish survive?

_____

_____

_____

Lesson 1: What are plants' characteristics?

Vocabulary

photosynthesis the process in which plants make their own food

chlorophyll green material in plants that captures energy from sunlight for photosynthesis

What Are the Parts of Plant Cells?

How is a giant redwood tree like a small dandelion? Both organisms belong to the plant kingdom. Both organisms are multi-celled. This means they are made of many cells.

All plants are made of cells. Cells are grouped together to make tissues and organs. Some cells make food. Each plant has special parts that absorb water and nutrients from the soil. These special parts use the energy from sunlight to change water and nutrients into food for the plant.

How Plants Make Food

All plants need sunlight and water. They also need carbon dioxide from the air and nutrients from the soil. They use these things to make food. The food they make is sugar. The process of making sugar is called **photosynthesis.**

Photosynthesis begins when a plant's roots take in water and nutrients from the soil. The water and nutrients travel through tubes in the plant's stem to its leaves. Then, the plant uses energy from the sun to change these things into sugar. This sugar is carried to other plant parts by the tubes in the stem. Extra sugar is stored in the stems, roots, and leaves. Oxygen and water are made during photosynthesis too. They are waste products. The plant passes these waste products into the air through openings in its leaves.

Chloroplasts

Photosynthesis happens in the chloroplasts of leaf cells. Chloroplasts have **chlorophyll** in them. Chlorophyll is what makes plants green. Chlorophyll also captures energy from sunlight. The plant uses this energy to make food.

Plant Habitats

Plants grow in many places. They have special adaptations that help them live. For example, water lilies grow at the bottom of ponds. Their stems reach up through the top of the water. Water lilies have large leaves that float on the water. These leaves trap energy from sunlight. This energy is used during photosynthesis.

© Pearson Education, Inc. 4

Name _____

Lesson 1 Review

Use with pp. 47–49

Lesson 1 Checkpoint

1. What is a multi-celled organism?

_____

_____

2. Name three characteristics of plants.

_____

_____

3. In what part of the plant cell does photosynthesis occur?

_____

_____

4. **Draw Conclusions** Most plant parts that are green contain chlorophyll. What might you conclude about a plant part that is not green?

_____

_____

© Pearson Education, Inc. 4

Quick Study

Chapter 2, Lesson 1 Review **13**

Lesson 2: What are the parts of plants?

The Roles of Leaves and Stems

Plants are made of many cells. Some cells make food. Other cells store the food. Groups of cells that work together are called tissue. Wood is one kind of plant tissue.

Different tissues work together to form organs. Leaves, stems, and roots are plant organs. Almost all plants have these organs.

All leaves have the same job. They make food. Leaves come in many shapes and sizes. This makes their job easier. For example, pine trees have thin, pointy needles. This shape keeps the trees from losing too much water. Most plants have flat leaves. This shape helps leaves collect sunlight. The plant uses the sunlight's energy to make food.

All stems have the same two jobs. They hold up the leaves. This helps them catch sunlight. Stems also carry water, minerals, and food through the plant.

Some stems are soft. You could bend them in your hand. These stems are usually green. They make food like leaves do. Daisies and tomato plants have soft, green stems. Woody stems are hard and thick. They hold up larger plants. Bark is a layer of dead cells. It protects these plants. Maple trees have hard, woody stems.

The Roles of Roots

Roots have many jobs. One job is to keep the plant in the ground. They also take in water and minerals from the soil. One job roots cannot do is make food. Root cells do not have chlorophyll in them. But some roots can store extra food. The plant uses this food when it cannot make enough during photosynthesis.

Roots grow away from the stem to find water and nutrients. A fibrous root system has roots growing in many directions. This lets the plant absorb water and minerals from a large area. Grasses and trees have fibrous roots. Their roots are long. They are not thick.

Taproots

A large, main root is called a taproot. A taproot grows straight down. The taproot stores water and nutrients from the soil. It grows thicker as it stores food for the plant. Carrots, turnips, and dandelions have taproots.

Root hairs grow out from the sides of the taproot. They take in water and nutrients from the soil. Root hairs help the plant get the materials it needs to grow and make food.

Plants Without Roots

Some plants do not have underground roots. They are called air plants. They absorb moisture from the air. They take nutrients from dust in the air. Air plants use these things to make their own food. Spanish moss is an air plant. It grows in many parts of the southern United States. It hangs from walls, fences, and other plants.

© Pearson Education, Inc. 4

Lesson 2 Checkpoint

1. Why do larger plants have woody instead of flexible stems?

_____

_____

2. What are two jobs of roots?

_____

_____

3. How do stems help a plant survive?

_____

_____

Lesson 3: How do plants reproduce?

Vocabulary

sepal one of several leaf-life parts that cover and protect the flower bud

pistil a female structure in plants that produces egg cells

stamen male structure in plants that makes pollen

ovary the thick bottom part of the pistil where the egg cells are stored

fertilization the process by which an egg cell and a sperm cell combine

Parts of Flowers

Biologists group plants by how they make new plants. One group makes seeds. Flowering plants and conifers are in this group.

Most flowers have four main parts. You can see a flower's petals easily. Petals are colorful. They come in many shapes and sizes. **Petals** help protect the part of the flower that makes seeds.

Sepals are the small green leaves that are below the petals. They protect the flower as it grows inside the bud.

The **pistil** is in the center of the flower. It is the female part of a flower. Pistils make egg cells. **Stamens** are the smaller stalks around the pistil. Stamens are the male part of a flower. They make pollen. The sperm in pollen joins with the flower's egg cells to make seeds.

Incomplete Flowers

Most flowers are made of the sepals, petals, stamens, and at least one pistil. But some flowers do not have all these parts. For example, a corn plant has two kinds of flowers. The corn tassel is one flower. It is a male flower that has stamens and no pistils. The corn silk is the other flower. It is a female flower that has pistils but no stamens. The sperm from the stamens join with the eggs in the pistil to make seeds.

Pollen on the Move

Pollen has to move from a stamen to a pistil for a seed to form. This movement is called pollination. The wind helps pollination happen. Plants that use the wind for pollination don't have sweet smells or colorful petals. They produce huge amounts of pollen instead. Then, the wind carries a few grains of pollen to another flower.

Animals can also help pollination happen. Animals come to flowers because of their bright colors and good smell. Flowers also make a sweet liquid called nectar. The animals have to reach deep into the flower to drink the nectar. Pollen rubs off onto the animal's body as it drinks. Then, the pollen may fall onto the pistil of the next flower the animal visits.

A thin tube begins to grow after pollen lands on a pistil. This tube grows down from the pollen grain through the pistil. The pollen tube reaches the **ovary** at the bottom of the pistil. Sperm cells from the pollen move down the pollen tube into the ovary. Then, the sperm and egg join in a process called **fertilization.**

Fertilization

After fertilization, the flower changes. The petals and stamens fall off. The fertilized egg grows into a seed. The ovary gets larger and turns into a fruit. The fruit protects the seed or seeds. Some fruit is soft and wet, like peaches or grapes. Other fruit is hard and dry, like peanut shells. The seeds are ready to grow into new plants when the fruit becomes ripe.

Lesson 3 Checkpoint

1. What are the four main parts of a flower?

_____

_____

_____

_____

2. What part of the flower makes egg cells?

_____

_____

3. What are some ways that pollen moves from stamen to pistil?

_____

_____

_____

_____

Lesson 4: What is the life cycle of a plant?

Vocabulary

dormant a state of rest

Life Cycle of a Flowering Plant

Plants have different life cycles. Some plants live for a short time. Others live for years.

A seed needs oxygen, water, sunlight, and temperature to grow, or germinate. The young plant inside the seed uses stored food to grow. Leaves will grow on the young plant. They will make food for the plant through photosynthesis. The young plant grows to be an adult plant. It gets larger and grows flowers.

The parent plant might make more flowers and seeds. Finally, this plant will die. Its death completes the life cycle.

Seeds on the Move

What would happen if cherries fell off a tree onto the ground? The cherries' seeds would start to grow. But the parent tree's roots would suck up most of the nutrients from the soil. Its leaves would let only a little sunlight reach the seeds. They would not have enough space or resources to grow. This is why plants have adaptations that help them scatter their seeds.

Fruit seeds have a special cover. Many animals eat fruit. The cover lets the seeds move through the animal's body without being hurt. The seeds end up in the animal's droppings. The droppings are far from the parent plant.

Some animals bury nuts and seeds. Some nuts and seeds grow after they are buried.

Dandelions and cottonwood trees have threads. They carry fruit and seeds. The wind carries these threads far away.

Water also moves fruit and seeds. Coconuts come from palm trees. They can float between islands. Storms wash the fruit onto a beach where a new palm tree can grow.

Starting to Grow

A seed holds a small plant. The seed gives the plant energy to start growing. The seed will stay **dormant** if it does not have what it needs. A seed can stay dormant for a long time.

Some plants do not make flowers or cones. They grow from spores instead of seeds. A spore is simpler than a seed. It is made of one cell. This means it has very little stored food. Like a seed, spores can stay dormant for years. Spores will grow into plants when they have water and the right temperature. Spores grow in spore cases. Spores fly into the air when their cases pop open. Some spores land near the parent plant. The wind carries the others away.

New Plants from Plant Parts

Some plants grow from stems, roots, or leaves. Other plants grow from bulbs. A bulb is an underground stem. It is made of thick layers of leaves. The leaves will turn green and make food when they grow out of the soil.

Some plants grow on the parent plant. Sprouts grow on potatoes. The sprouts will grow into new potato plants.

Strawberry plants have stems called runners. Roots grow from the runners into the soil. They make new plants.

Some plants grow from the stems of other plants. For example, you could cut the stem of an African violet plant and place it in water. A new African violet plant would grow. These pieces are called cuttings. They can be taken from roots and leaves too.

Lesson 4 Checkpoint

1. What does a seed need to germinate?

_____

_____

2. Why is it important that seeds are scattered away from their parent plant?

_____

_____

3. Describe how spores are different from seeds.

_____

_____

_____

4. What are some ways that plants reproduce without seeds?

_____

_____

_____

5. Explain why death is a part of the life cycle of a plant.

_____

_____

6. 🎯 **Draw Conclusions** A healthy plant has water on the underside of several of its leaves. What can you conclude is the source of the water?

_____

_____

Name _____

Lesson 1: What are the parts of ecosystems?

Vocabulary

> **ecosystem** all the living and nonliving things in an environment and the many ways they interact
>
> **population** all the members of one species that live within an area of an ecosystem
>
> **community** different populations that interact with each other in the same area
>
> **niche** the specific role an organism has in its habitat

What a System Is

A system is made of many parts that work together. A system can have living and nonliving parts. An example of a simple system is a bicycle and rider. All the parts of the bike work together. For example, the handlebars steer the bike. Most systems need things added from outside the system to work. A bike needs a rider's actions to make it go. Systems also leave something behind, like dust. Each part in a system is important. If a part is missing, the system will not work as well.

An **ecosystem** is a system of living and nonliving things that interact with each other. Animals and plants are the living parts. Nonliving parts of an ecosystem are sand, air, water, sunlight, and soil.

Grasslands, deserts, and tundra are ecosystems. Grasslands are covered with tall grasses. They get medium rain. Deserts are very dry. The desert is also very hot. The tundra is dry and cold. The ground is frozen all year.

Organisms and Environment

Living things, like plants and animals, are called organisms. Organisms can live only if they meet their needs. For example, plants and animals in a desert know how to conserve water and stay cool.

A **population** is all the members of one kind of plant or animal. All the birds in the desert make up the population of birds. The size of each population may change depending on how much food, water, and space is in an ecosystem.

A **community** is all the different populations in an ecosystem. Each population interacts with others. All the plants and animals in a desert ecosystem are a community.

The place where an organism lives in an ecosystem is called its habitat. It is the organism's "home" and contains everything that the organism needs to live.

Special Roles

Each organism in an ecosystem has a job or role called an organism's **niche.** For example, a roadrunner's niche includes hunting for snakes. Every population in a habitat has a different niche.

Name _____

Lesson 1 Checkpoint

1. What are some nonliving parts of an ecosystem?

_____

_____

2. Describe three ecosystems.

_____

_____

_____

3. Describe the living and nonliving parts of an ecosystem.

_____

_____

4. Explain the difference between an organism's habitat and its niche.

_____

_____

Name _____

Lesson 2: How does energy flow in ecosystems?

Vocabulary

herbivores consumers that get energy by eating only plants

carnivores consumers that eat only animals

omnivores consumers that eat both plants and animals

decomposers organisms that eat the waste and remains of dead plants and animals

Energy in Plants and Animals

Sunlight is energy for life on Earth. Plants use sunlight to make their own food. This is called photosynthesis. Plants are called producers because they make their own food. Most organisms cannot make their own food. They need to eat other organisms. These organisms are called consumers.

There are different kinds of consumers. **Herbivores** are consumers that eat only plants. A deer is an herbivore. **Carnivores** eat only other animals. Mountain lions are carnivores. **Omnivores**, such as roadrunners, eat both plants and animals. Consumers like turkey vultures eat only dead plants and animals. They are called scavengers.

A Food Chain

A food chain begins with energy from sunlight. Producers, like plants, are next in the chain. Plants like the prickly pear cactus make food from sunlight. Then an animal eats the cactus. For example, in a desert ecosystem the collared peccary is an omnivore. It eats producers, like the prickly pear cactus. Coyotes are carnivores. They hunt and kill animals, like the collared peccary, to eat them.

Every time an organism eats something, the energy is passed on. The energy from sunlight is passed to the prickly pear cactus. Then it is passed to the collared peccary when it eats the cactus. The energy is passed to the coyote when it eats the collared peccary.

Decomposers Are Important

The food chain needs more than producers and consumers. If there were only producers, plants would soon use all the minerals in the soil. The plants would die. Then herbivores would not have any food.

Dead plants and animals still have energy inside them. **Decomposers** like bacteria and fungi eat dead plants and animals. The tiny decomposers break down the tissues into minerals and nutrients. These go into the soil. Plants need these to make food. When animals eat the plants, the energy moves along the food chain.

A Food Web

An ecosystem has many food chains. The same food source can be part of more than one food chain. This means that one food chain can overlap another food chain.

For example, coyotes and mountain lions are both carnivores. They both hunt prey like the collared peccary. When food chains overlap, there is a food web.

© Pearson Education, Inc. 4

Quick Study

Lesson 2 Checkpoint

1. Describe three types of consumers.

_____

2. Name animals from the food web on page 89 of your textbook that are carnivores.

_____

_____

3. Why are fungi and bacteria important to energy transfer in an ecosystem?

_____

_____

4. Why are decomposers important in the food chain?

_____

_____

5. ⦿ **Sequence** Look at this food chain. grass⟶grasshopper⟶ mouse⟶snake⟶hawk. Make a flow chart that shows how energy stored by grass is transferred to the hawk.

Name _____

Lesson 3: How does matter flow in ecosystems?

Water Ecosystems

Almost three-fourths of Earth's surface is covered with water. Many organisms live in water ecosystems. Water ecosystems can be in shallow water or deep water. They can be saltwater or freshwater.

The Okefenokee Swamp is a freshwater ecosystem. It is wet all year. In a swamp ecosystem, producers can be as small as a single-celled algae or as large as a tree. It is home to many plants animals, and fish.

How Matter Flows Through a Food Web

Energy and matter move through a food web. Matter is anything that has mass and takes up space. In a swamp ecosystem, many producers and consumers are part of more than one food chain. The Okefenokee Swamp is in south Georgia and north Florida. One producer in the swamp is algae. Algae gets energy from sunlight, like a plant. But algae does not make its own food like a plant does. Algae gets nutrients from the water.

The freshwater snail is a consumer in a swamp ecosystem. It eats algae. The sandhill crane and the Great Blue Heron eat freshwater snails. These birds get some of the matter they need by eating snails.

Decay in Ecosystems

All living things eventually die. After they die, they begin to decay. Decay is very important in an ecosystem. Without decay, dead organisms would pile up and get in the way of living things.

During decay, scavengers eat the remains of dead organisms. Decomposers like fungi and bacteria break down the dead organisms. This returns minerals and nutrients to the ecosystem.

Rate of Decay

Dead organisms can decay slowly or quickly. How fast an organism decays depends on temperature. In colder temperatures decay happens more slowly. In hot temperatures decay happens quickly.

Fungi and bacteria need oxygen to live and grow. More oxygen makes decay happen faster. Usually decay happens faster when there is more moisture.

Quick Study

© Pearson Education, Inc. 4

Lesson 3 Checkpoint

1. Describe some freshwater ecosystem.

_____

_____

2. The producer in the Okefenokee Swamp food web on pages 92–93 of your textbook is not a plant. Explain how this is possible.

_____

_____

3. Name some things that affect how fast an organism decays.

_____

_____

_____

4. Explain why decay might happen more quickly in summer months than in winter months.

_____

_____

5. **Sequence** Draw a flowchart that shows how the food energy stored in algae is tansferred to the osprey.

Lesson 1: How are ecosystems balanced?

Needs of Living Things

The Eastern American chipmunk lives in the Great Smoky Mountains. It needs living and nonliving things in the forest. The chipmunk gets food from plants. Plants also give the chipmunk oxygen. It needs oxygen to breathe. The chipmunk drinks water from puddles and streams. It digs its hole near the bottom of a tree. The hole protects the chipmunk from cold weather and other animals.

All plants and animals need food, water, space, shelter, light, and air to grow and be healthy. Organisms also need the right soil and weather. Living things get what they need from their environment.

A Balancing Act

An ecosystem is made of organisms that live in the same environment. The organisms need each other to live. What happens to one population affects the community.

An ecosystem is healthy when it is balanced. An ecosystem is balanced when all the animals living in it have food. When the population increases, food may run out. There will not be enough food if there are too many animals. This means the ecosystem is not balanced.

An ecosystem of plants can be balanced too. The ecosystem is balanced when each plant gets what it needs. Plants need minerals from the soil, water, and sunlight. Plants also need space. If you plant tree seeds close together, many of the seeds will not grow. They will not have enough space to grow into trees. The ecosystem is out of balance when plants don't get what they need.

All organisms help keep an ecosystem balanced. For example, rabbits eat grass. This keeps the grass from taking space other plants need. Red foxes eat rabbits. The foxes keep the number of rabbits from getting too large. It also keeps too much grass from being eaten. The grass creates oxygen. Animals need the oxygen to breathe.

© Pearson Education, Inc. 4

Lesson 1 Checkpoint

1. What do all plants and animals need to live and grow?

_____

_____

2. What happens when the number of organisms in a population increases?

_____

_____

3. What are two things that might prevent a plant population from growing in size?

_____

_____

Lesson 2: How do organisms interact?

Vocabulary

competition when two or more species in an ecosystem must use the same limited resources

parasite an organism that lives on or in another organism, helping itself but hurting the other organism

host an organism that is harmed by a parasite

Change in Ecosystems

Changes help keep ecosystems in balance. For example, animals use the oxygen in an ecosystem. But new plants put oxygen back into the ecosystem.

Populations in an ecosystem change. Organisms need resources, like food and water. Think about the chipmunk at the beginning of the chapter. Chipmunk populations grow where there is a lot of food. More food, water, and space are needed when a population grows. A larger chipmunk population may use up many of these resources.

Each chipmunk gets less food, water, and space when there are fewer resources. Some chipmunks will die. Others will move to a new place. This means there are more resources for the chipmunks that stay. Then, the population increases.

Competing and Sharing

Populations can grow when they get what they need. But populations that live in the same ecosystem may need the same resources. This is called **competition.** Organisms have to compete for resources. Organisms that compete well live longer and have offspring.

Populations compete for living space. Different plants compete for light and water. Birds compete for the same place to build a nest. Foxes and owls compete for animals to eat.

Animals also behave in ways to avoid competition. For example, both hawks and owls eat some of the same animals. Hawks and owls hunt for food at different times to reduce competition. Hawks hunt during the day. Owls hunt at night.

Living in groups can make it easier for animals to get food or stay safe. Wolves hunt for animals like deer. Wolves work together to hunt a deer. Deer travel in groups to protect themselves. This makes it hard for wolves to attack any one deer.

Living Side by Side

Two different organisms can live together. Sometimes living together can help both organisms. For example, fungi and algae live together on rocks. The algae give sugar, food, and water to the fungi. The fungi protect the algae. They guard the algae from too much sun and very warm weather.

Sometimes living together helps one organism but hurts the other. The organism that is helped is called a **parasite.** Parasites live on or in another organism, called the **host.** The host is harmed by the parasite. A parasite uses its host for food. For example, mistletoe is a parasite plant. It grows on oak trees. Mistletoe takes food and water away from its host tree.

Name _____

Lesson 2 Checkpoint

1. What are two behaviors that help animals to avoid or reduce competition?

   _____

   _____

2. **Cause and Effect** Identify the cause and effect of deer traveling in groups.

   _____

   _____

3. What is a parasite?

   _____

   _____

4. What might happen to the parasite if its host were to die?

   _____

   _____

Lesson 3: How do environments change?

Vocabulary

succession gradual change from one community of organisms to another

extinct an entire species is extinct if it has died out and is gone forever

endangered a species is endangered if it is in danger of becoming extinct

The Process of Change

Thousands of years ago, a forest may have been a lake. After many years, the lake dried up and became a marsh. Then trees grew where the marsh used to be. These changes from one kind of environment to another are called **succession.** Succession happens as the environment changes.

Changes in climate may affect ecosystems. Climate is the average temperature and rainfall in an area over many years. Climates change slowly. Over 15,000 years ago, snow and ice covered parts of North America. Trees and plants could not grow. Then, the climate became warmer. Plants and animals moved in. This formed today's forest communities.

Changing Species

In the 1800s and early 1900s, there were many passenger pigeons. By 1915, all the passenger pigeons had died. The passenger pigeon was **extinct.** This means the entire species died out and was gone forever. Species become extinct because they cannot adapt to changes in Earth's environment. Climate changes, volcanoes, and meteors have caused extinction. Now humans are the main reason a species becomes extinct. People hunt animals and destroy their habitats.

The populations of some species have become very small. They are called **endangered** species. They are in danger of becoming extinct. Species that may soon become endangered are called threatened species.

Species Then and Now

Scientists study the remains of animals and plants from long ago. These remains are called fossils. Scientists compare fossils of organisms that lived long ago to organisms that are alive today. Scientists learn how species have changed or adapted to the environment and climate.

Fossils tell us about the environment long ago. Scientists have found the fossils of water organisms in dry climates. This means that long ago, shallow water covered the area where they were found.

Rapid Natural Changes

Hurricanes, floods, fires, volcanic eruptions, and earthquakes are natural events. They quickly change the land. These changes may force species to leave the area because they cannot get the resources they need.

Rapid events also help ecosystems stay balanced. For example, fires clear away dead plants. This leaves room for new plants.

A Great Flood

In 1993, rain caused the Mississippi and Missouri Rivers to overflow. Some areas were flooded for almost 200 days. Many acres of land were covered with sand and mud.

The floods affected many plants and animals. Grasses and trees died because there was too much water. Many birds had fewer babies because their nests were destroyed. Some fish could eat and reproduce in the flooded areas. Their populations grew.

Quick Study

Lesson 3 Checkpoint

1. What is succession?

_____

_____

2. When are species considered threatened?

_____

_____

3. **Cause and Effect** Why do organisms become extinct?

_____

_____

_____

4. Name two processes that change an environment over a very long period of time.

_____

_____

5. What are two events that change an environment very quickly?

_____

_____

Name _____

Lesson 4: How do people disturb the balance?

Vocabulary

hazardous wastes substances that are very harmful to humans and other organisms

People and the Environment

Humans get food, shelter, and water from the land. Humans can also change the environment to meet their needs. For example, we cut down trees to get wood. This also gives us space to build houses. We clear fields to plant crops or build roads. These changes can upset the balance of ecosystems.

Products we make and use also affect ecosystems. Wastes from these products can pollute the air and water. For example, harmful chemicals from automobiles and factories pollute the air. These chemicals can hurt plants. Animals that eat these plants lose food. Animals that live on or near these plants lose shelter.

Wastes and chemicals get into rivers, lakes, and oceans. This pollutes the water. Some wastes come from sewer systems. Other chemicals are used on land. They help plants grow or kill bugs. Rain washes these chemicals into the water. Some of these chemicals can hurt or kill fish, plants, and animals. Another pollutant is oil. Sometimes oil spills when it is shipped or drilled. The oil covers algae, plants, mollusks, and fish. This makes them die. Birds covered in oil often drown.

Land Pollution

Garbage can pollute the land. Humans make a lot of garbage. Most trash is taken to a landfill and covered with dirt.

Hazardous wastes are also pollutants. They can be very dangerous to animals and humans. They can also start fires or cause diseases. Hazardous wastes used to be buried in the ground. They hurt nearby habitats.

Stripping Away the Land

Coal is a valuable substance. It is under the Earth's surface. Strip mining is one way to get coal. Huge machines used to dig large holes in the soil. The land around the holes washed away. Soil and rock were washed into ponds and rivers. Nearby ecosystems were greatly affected.

Land Reclamation

Now mining companies must replace the rock and soil they take away. They must also replant trees and grasses. This helps animals return to their habitats. Crops can be planted.

Preserving the Environment

The United States has created National Parks to protect land. These parks also protect the habitats of many plants and animals.

Yellowstone National Park was the first national park in the world. It is mostly in Wyoming. You can see geysers in Yellowstone. Geysers are springs that shoot hot water high into the air.

The Saguaro National Park is covered with cactuses. It is a home for many desert plants and animals. This park also protects very old villages.

© Pearson Education, Inc. 4

Lesson 4 Checkpoint

1. Why do humans have a great impact on the environment?

_____

_____

_____

_____

2. What human activities damage the environment?

_____

_____

3. What are some of the effects of habitat destruction?

_____

_____

4. What are some things people have done to protect the environment?

_____

_____

Lesson 1: What are the skeletal and muscular systems?

Vocabulary

voluntary muscles muscles that you control

involuntary muscles muscles that you cannot control

Parts of Organ Systems

Your body is made of many kinds of cells. Similar cells work together to form tissues.

Tissues form organs. They help you live. Each organ in your body has a different job. For example, your heart is an organ. It has muscle, nerve, and connecting tissues that work together to pump blood.

A group of organs that work together makes up an organ system. The heart and blood vessels are organs. They make up the circulatory system. Each part of an organ system is important. If one organ doesn't work, it affects the other organs in the system.

Organ systems work together. For example, your skeletal and muscle systems work together to help you stand and skate.

The Skeletal System

Bones are made of tissue. They make up your skeleton. It holds up your body. Without it, you would fall into a pile on the floor.

Your skeleton also protects organs inside your body, like the brain, heart, and lungs. Muscles that move your body are attached to your skeleton. This helps you move.

Many bones in your skeleton also make blood cells. Some of these blood cells carry oxygen to other cells. Other cells fight germs that could make you sick. Some cells stop bleeding.

Your skeletal system needs minerals to stay healthy. Calcium is a mineral. It helps keep bones strong. Your bones hold calcium in case your body needs it later.

Types of Joints

Joints hold your bones together and allow them to move. A joint is the place where one bone attaches to another.

A ball-and-socket joint is made of one bone that fits into another bone. It lets your bones move in a circle, as when you are swinging your arm.

A hinge joint lets your bones move backward or forward. One hinge joint lets you bend or straighten your knee.

The Muscular System

Muscles move your body. They are attached to your skeleton. Without muscles, you could not move, breathe, or swallow.

Some muscles are **voluntary muscles.** You can choose when you want these muscles to move. You use voluntary muscles when you smile, run, and chew.

Most muscles in your body are skeletal muscles. These muscles are voluntary. Skeletal muscles work in pairs. When you bend your arm, one muscle tightens. The other becomes loose. When you straighten your arm, the first muscle loosens. The second muscle tightens.

Muscles that you cannot control are called **involuntary muscles.** You use involuntary muscles when you breathe or digest food. These muscles are also in blood vessels. They help to keep blood flowing.

Your body has two kinds of involuntary muscle tissue: smooth muscles and cardiac muscles. Cardiac muscles are only in your heart. Smooth muscles are in different organs of your body. The systems in your body could not do their jobs without smooth muscle.

© Pearson Education, Inc. 4

Lesson 1 Checkpoint

1. Order the following from smallest to largest: organs, cells, organ systems, tissues.

_____

_____

2. Name four things that the skeletal system does.

_____

_____

_____

3. How do the skeletal and muscular systems work together?

_____

_____

_____

_____

4. What type of muscle tissue would you find in the heart? blood vessels? toes?

_____

_____

5. **Draw Conclusions** You read about some of the jobs of the involuntary muscles. Why is it important for these muscles to work without your control?

_____

_____

Lesson 2: What are the respiratory and circulatory systems?

The Respiratory System

Your body needs oxygen to do everything. Your respiratory system brings oxygen to your body. Air enters your body through your nose and mouth. Then it moves through your pharynx, or throat. It goes on to your trachea, or windpipe. The trachea divides into two branches. Each branch is called a bronchial tube. Each bronchial tube connects to tiny air sacs in the lung.

Tiny blood vessels are wrapped around each air sac. Oxygen from the air sacs passes into the blood through these vessels. This blood carries oxygen to your body's cells.

Take a Breath!

Your body cells give off carbon dioxide when they use oxygen. The respiratory system helps move these gases in and out of your body.

The lungs are the main organs in the respiratory system. But the lungs don't have muscles, so how can they move? A diaphragm is a muscle. It sits under your lungs. Air is forced in and out of your lungs when your diaphragm moves. You breathe in and out.

How Pumps and Passages Work Together

Your respiratory system works with your circulatory system to bring oxygen to cells and carry carbon dioxide away from cells. Your heart, blood vessels, and blood are the main parts of your circulatory system. The circulatory system's job is to move blood through the body. The blood brings oxygen to the body's cells.

Each breath you take brings oxygen into your respiratory system. Oxygen from the air sacs in your lungs goes into your blood. Blood vessels carry this blood to your heart.

The right and left sides of the heart work like pumps. Each pump has two parts. One part is the atrium. The other part is the ventricle.

The left atrium of your heart collects the blood from the lungs. This blood is full of oxygen. It moves from the left atrium into the left ventricle. Then, the heart pumps this blood to the rest of the body.

The right atrium collects blood from the body. This blood is full of carbon dioxide. It needs oxygen. The blood moves from the right atrium to the right ventricle. Then, the blood is pumped to your lungs. The carbon dioxide leaves your body when you breathe out.

A muscle wall separates the heart's pumps. It does not allow blood going to the heart to mix with blood leaving the heart.

Lesson 2 Checkpoint

1. Describe how oxygen from the air gets to the cells of your body.

_____

_____

2. Name the three main parts of the circulatory system.

_____

_____

3. Explain why it is important to move blood through the body.

_____

_____

Lesson 3: What are the digestive and nervous systems?

Vocabulary

neuron basic working unit of the nervous system or the nerve cell

The Digestive System

Food that you eat must be broken down into nutrients your cells can use. This is called digestion. Digestion happens as the foods you eat move through your digestive system.

Digestion begins in your mouth. Your teeth and saliva start to break down food. Then you swallow it. The food enters a tube called the esophagus. Then it moves into your stomach. The muscles in your stomach crush the food. It gets mixed with juices from your stomach walls. The food turns into a thick liquid. This liquid moves into a folded tube. This tube is your small intestine. The food will stay in the small intestine for three to six hours. The small intestine and other organs break the food down into nutrients. The nutrients pass through thin blood vessels in the intestine. Blood carries the nutrients to body cells.

The Central Nervous System

Your central nervous system is the control center of your body. Your brain and spinal cord make up your central nervous system. This system links all your body systems. It carries signals from one system to another. Your central nervous system controls your breathing and heart rate. It also controls how your skeletal and smooth muscles move.

The central nervous system also gets information about changes that happen outside your body. Your sense organs get this information. Your eyes, ears, nose, and tongue are your sense organs. The central nervous system sends messages to different body systems so you can react. For example, if a friend yells "Catch!" your ears hear the sound. You see the ball, reach out, and grab it. These actions happen because your central nervous system sends signals to many body parts.

The spinal cord connects the parts of the central nervous system. Signals between your brain and body parts pass along your spinal cord. Sometimes the spinal cord controls your body. It controls your reflexes. Reflexes are actions that you don't think about. Blinking is a reflex.

Neurons

The brain is an organ. It is made of billions of nerve cells. These cells are called **neurons.** Your spinal cord is made of many neurons. Neurons carry information through your central nervous system.

Lesson 3 Checkpoint

1. Where does the process of digestion begin?

_____

_____

2. What are the organs of the central nervous system?

_____

_____

3. Explain how the nervous, muscular, respiratory, and circulatory
systems work together to help you ride a bike.

_____

_____

_____

_____

_____

_____

Name _____

Lesson 4: How does the body defend itself?

Vocabulary

pathogens organisms that cause disease

infectious disease a disease that can pass from one organism to another

immune system the organs in your body that defend against disease

vaccine an injection of dead or weakened pathogens that causes you to be immune to a disease

Microorganisms in Your Body

When you get a cut, you should clean it and cover it with a bandage. This keeps it from getting infected. You get an infection when organisms with disease enter and grow in your body. Most organisms are so small that you can only see them with a microscope. They are called microorganisms.

Not all microorganisms in your body cause disease. Microorganisms are in your body all the time. They are on your skin, in your mouth, and in your digestive system.

Your Body's Defenses

Your body has special cells, tissues, organs, and chemicals. They protect you from microorganisms. Your skin, mouth, and stomach are organs that protect your body from disease.

Your skin covers and protects your body. Your sweat has acids that kill many microorganisms that can cause disease.

Your body has other ways to protect itself. For example, your tears wash away or kill microorganisms that could cause disease in your eyes. Mucus and saliva in your mouth wash away microorganisms that can cause disease.

Bacteria and Viruses

Pathogens are organisms that cause disease. They create an infection if they enter and grow in your body. Diseases caused by pathogens are infectious. An **infectious**

disease is a disease that you can pass on to someone else.

There are many kinds of pathogens. Bacteria and viruses are pathogens. Some viruses get into the cells of your nose, mouth, and throat. These viruses give you a cold.

Staying Healthy

Some microorganisms that cause disease travel through the air. This is why you should cover your mouth and nose when you sneeze or cough. Diseases can travel between two people. They can also travel between a person and an object. There are things you can do to stay healthy. Wash your hands before you eat. Make sure that objects other people have used are clean before you use them. Things like towels, glasses, and silverware can pass microorganisms with diseases from one person to another.

Attacking the Invaders

Your **immune system** helps protect you against many pathogens. It is made of blood cells and other tissues. Special white blood cells work together to destroy pathogens. These white blood cells also make antibodies. An antibody is a chemical your body makes to stop pathogens from infecting other cells.

A **vaccine** is a kind of medicine that protects you from disease. This protection is called immunity. The vaccine causes your immune system to make antibodies against a certain kind of pathogen.

© Pearson Education, Inc. 4

Lesson 4 Checkpoint

1. What are some of your body's defenses against invading microorganisms?

   _____

   _____

2. 🎯 **Draw Conclusions** Use the facts on pages 156–157 to draw conclusions about ways to prevent some diseases.

   _____

   _____

3. What is an infectious disease?

   _____

   _____

4. What are antibodies?

   _____

   _____

5. Explain how a vaccine causes immunity.

   _____

   _____

Lesson 1: Where is Earth's water?

Earth—The Water Planet

Did you know 3/4 of Earth's surface is covered with water? Water is needed for life. Organisms live in water. Water also gives organisms food.

Earth's water is found in three forms. It can be a liquid. Water can also freeze into ice at a temperature of 0°C. Finally, water can turn into a gas called water vapor at 100° C.

Over 97/100 of Earth's water is in the oceans and seas. Less than 1/100 of Earth's water is in lakes and rivers. The rest, over 2/100 of Earth's water, is frozen in glaciers and ice caps.

Salty Water

Have you ever tasted ocean water? It tastes salty. Ocean water is not healthy to drink. Your body cannot use this water.

Water is made of hydrogen and oxygen. Ocean water is made of water and small solids. The salt in ocean water comes from rocks and soils on land. Rivers break down the salts. Rivers carry these salts to the ocean.

Differences in Saltiness

Some oceans are saltier than others. In warm places, ocean water quickly turns into water vapor. Salt is left behind. It makes the water very salty. The Red Sea has deserts on three sides. It has some of the saltiest water on Earth.

In cool places, ocean water turns into water vapor slowly. This makes ocean water near the North and South Poles less salty. Oceans are also less salty in places where water flows from rivers. Many rivers flow into the Baltic Sea. This makes its water less salty than average.

Most of Earth's water is salty ocean water. Most of Earth's fresh water is frozen in glaciers and ice caps. Liquid fresh water is underground. It is also in lakes, rivers, and streams. Fresh water also comes from snow and rain.

© Pearson Education, Inc. 4

Lesson 1 Checkpoint

1. About how much of Earth's water is frozen in glaciers and ice caps?

   _____

2. Why is water in the Baltic Sea less salty than most ocean water?

   _____

   _____

3. Is the water in the Red Sea more or less salty than average?

   _____

4. 🎯 **Cause and Effect** What causes ocean water to be more salty than average in warm places?

   _____

   _____

   _____

Lesson 2: How do water and air affect weather?

Vocabulary

evaporation the process of changing liquid water to water vapor

condensation the process of water vapor becoming liquid water when it cools

precipitation any form of water that falls to Earth

How Water Is Recycled

Earth's water is always being recycled. Water moves from Earth's surface to its atmosphere. Then, it moves from the atmosphere back to the surface. This movement is called the water cycle.

Have you ever seen a puddle after it rains? Some water may run into a drain. Some water may run into the ground. The rest of the water goes into the air. Water is made of moving particles. They rise when the Sun's energy warms the water. The particles change into a gas called water vapor. This process is called **evaporation**.

Water vapor cools when it rises. This causes the water vapor to turn back into water. This is called **condensation**. This water forms clouds.

A cloud is made of tiny drops of water. These drops join together. They become too heavy for the cloud to hold. Then, they fall as **precipitation**. The water cycle begins again.

The Earth's Atmosphere

The air around the Earth is the atmosphere. Air is made of different gases. Most of Earth's atmosphere is nitrogen. Oxygen and carbon dioxide are also in the atmosphere. Water vapor is found in the part of the atmosphere closest to Earth. The amount of water vapor in the air depends on time and place. For example, air over an ocean will have more water vapor than air over a desert.

Air Pressure

Gravity presses air towards Earth's surface. The force of this air is called air pressure. Air pressure decreases as you go higher in the atmosphere.

Temperature also affects air pressure. An area of low pressure forms when air near the Earth's surface warms. The air particles move farther apart. This allows the air to rise. Then, the air pushes down with less pressure.

An area of high pressure forms when air near the Earth's surface cools. The air particles move closer together. This air sinks. It makes warm air rise.

Air moves from an area with high pressure to an area with low pressure. This moving air is called wind. Wind is named by the direction it comes from. A north wind comes from the north. It blows toward the south.

Quick Study

Lesson 2 Checkpoint

1. What is the water cycle?

_____

_____

2. What happens when water vapor cools?

_____

3. What happens to air pressure as you go higher in the atmosphere?

_____

4. **Cause and Effect** How do differences in air pressure cause wind?

_____

_____

_____

Name _____

Lesson 3: What are air masses?

Vocabulary

humidity the amount of water vapor in the air

front the area where two different air masses meet

Air Masses

An air mass is a large body of air. It has about the same temperature and **humidity** throughout. Air masses move and meet. This causes most weather. Air masses form over large areas of land or water. These areas heat or cool the air mass.

The area an air mass covers produces water vapor. Humidity is the amount of water vapor in the air. An ocean produces a lot of water vapor. An air mass that forms over an ocean will have high humidity. A desert is dry. It does not produce a lot of water vapor. An air mass that forms over a desert will have low humidity.

Air masses carry their temperature and humidity to other places. Meteorologists study air masses. This helps them predict the weather.

When Air Masses Meet: Cold Front

A **front** is the place where two different air masses meet. A cold front forms when a cold air mass meets a warm air mass. The pressure of cold air is higher than the pressure of warm air. The cold air sinks under the warm air. The warm air cools as it is pushed upward. Water vapor in the air condenses into clouds.

The colder air mass replaces the warmer air mass. Cold fronts can cause strong winds. They can cause heavy precipitation. Cold fronts usually move faster than warm fronts. This means the precipitation does not last very long. The colder air mass replaces the warmer air mass. The weather becomes cooler.

When Air Masses Meet: Warm Front

A warm front forms when a warm air mass meets a slower moving cold air mass. The warm air moves over the cold air mass. It cools as it rises. Water vapor in this air condenses. Cirrus clouds form.

Warm fronts usually move slower than cold fronts. The air spreads out more. This affects weather over a larger area. Stratus clouds form as the front passes through. They drop precipitation for a long time.

Cumulus clouds form when the skies clear. Air temperatures are usually higher after a warm front passes.

Clouds

The Sun's energy warms water on Earth. The heated water turns into water vapor. The air holding the water vapor rises and cools. The water vapor turns into water droplets and ice crystals. This causes clouds to form.

Scientists name clouds by their size, shape, and color. Conditions in the atmosphere control what a cloud is like. There are three basic kinds of clouds: cumulus, stratus, and cirrus. Cumulus clouds are thick, white, and puffy. They look like cotton. Sometimes, they appear in good weather. Stratus clouds are flat layers of clouds. They are close to Earth's surface. Cirrus clouds are feathery. They form high in the atmosphere.

© Pearson Education, Inc. 4

Lesson 3 Checkpoint

1. Why does an air mass that forms over a desert have low humidity?

   _____

   _____

2. What is an air mass?

   _____

3. Weather is caused by variations in what three basic ingredients?

   _____

   _____

   _____

4. **Cause and Effect** How does the Sun help cause clouds to form?

   _____

   _____

   _____

Name _____

Lesson 4 Summary

Use with pp. 194–199

Lesson 4: How do we measure and predict weather?

Vocabulary

meteorologists scientists who study and measure weather conditions

barometer a tool that measures air pressure

anemometer a tool that measures wind speed

wind vane a tool that shows the direction from which the wind is blowing

Measuring Weather

Changes in temperature, air, and water cause weather. **Meteorologists** measure these conditions to understand weather. Meteorologists use a thermometer to measure temperature. They use a **barometer** to measure air pressure.

An **anemometer** measures wind speed. The wind speed is high when the anemometer moves fast. A **wind vane** shows the direction from which the wind is blowing.

Meteorologists use a rain gauge to measure the amount of rainfall. They also use a hygrometer to measure the humidity in the air.

Predicting Weather

Meteorologists measure weather conditions over a large area. These measurements are used to find high and low pressure areas and fronts. Then, meteorologists make weather forecasts. A weather forecast predicts the weather for the next few days.

Meteorologists also use computer models. Weather radar watches where rain is falling. This helps forecast where rain will fall next.

Reading Weather Maps

Meteorologists use charts and maps to record measurements. Charts record daily weather measurements. A weather map uses symbols to show weather conditions. Curving lines connect places with the same air pressure. The letters *H* and *L* show high and low pressure areas. Triangles show cold fronts. Half circles show warm fronts.

How Weather and Climate Have Changed

Earth's climate has had very cold periods and warm periods. Now, Earth is in a warm period.

Scientists learn about Earth's climate in different ways. They cut into glaciers and learn what the climate was like when the ice formed. They also study tree rings. Each ring shows one year's growth. Scientists also look at the Earth's crust and guess when each layer of crust formed.

Earth's temperature and climate change slowly. Scientists think people cause some temperature changes. People burn fossil fuels. This makes a gas called carbon dioxide. It goes into the atmosphere. Too many gases can make Earth's temperature rise. Small rises in temperature can cause climates to change.

© Pearson Education, Inc. 4

Name _____

Lesson 4 Checkpoint

1. What does a barometer measure?

_____

2. How are curving lines used on a weather map?

_____

_____

3. **Infer** How can scientists today learn about Earth's past climate?

_____

_____

_____

© Pearson Education, Inc. 4

Lesson 1: What are hurricanes?

Vocabulary

hurricane a dangerous tropical storm with wind speeds of at least 119 kilometers per hour

tropical depression a tropical storm with wind speeds that swirl and can move up to 61 kilometers per hour

tropical storm storm that forms when wind speeds blow faster than 62 kilometers per hour

storm surge rise in sea level pushing large ocean waves onto shore; caused by storm's winds

How Tropical Storms Become Hurricanes

Tropical storms form in the tropics, a part of Earth near the equator. A **hurricane** is a dangerous storm with wind speeds of at least 119 kilometers per hour.

Stages of Tropical Storms

Tropical storms form over a large area of warm ocean water. These storms also need an area of low air pressure at the ocean surface. Winds blow from all directions to this area of low pressure. Winds carry heat and water vapor from the ocean. This warm, wet air rises. Clouds begin to form. Sometimes, these clouds become thunderstorms. Air in the thunderstorms gets warmer. The winds begin to move faster, becoming a **tropical depression**. Winds move up to 61 kilometers per hour in a tropical depression. It becomes a **tropical storm** when the winds blow faster than 62 kilometers per hour.

Hurricane as a System

A tropical storm becomes a hurricane when the winds reach 119 kilometers per hour. It is made of two systems that work together, the atmosphere and the ocean. A hurricane forms in the atmosphere and gets its energy from the warm ocean. Hurricanes can affect land and living things. A hurricane can cause floods and destroy homes.

The Hurricane's Eye

The area in the middle of a hurricane is called the eye. There are bands of thunderstorms around the eye. These storms have the strongest winds and rains. Inside the eye, winds are gentle and there is no rain.

The Effects of Winds and Water

A hurricane can cause much damage. Its winds can pick up and throw things. The winds can also break tree trunks and lift roofs off houses. Water causes the worst damage. A lot of rain falls as a hurricane moves over land, causing floods and mudslides.

A hurricane's winds can also push large waves of ocean water onto shore. This is called a **storm surge.** It can carry boats onto land and also cause major floods.

Sometimes, a hurricane can be helpful. The rains provide plants and wells with water, and also help prevent wildfires.

How Scientists Predict Hurricanes

Satellites above Earth collect information about a hurricane's rainfall. Special planes are used to fly into a hurricane and collect data about wind speed and water temperature. Scientists use this data to make computer models of the hurricane. They predict the speed, strength, and direction of a hurricane.

© Pearson Education, Inc. 4

Lesson 1 Checkpoint

1. How fast are a hurricane's winds?

   _____

2. What is the source of a hurricane's energy?

   _____

3. What are three ways in which a hurricane can cause damage?

   _____

   _____

   _____

4. How do weather satellites help people study hurricanes?

   _____

   _____

5. What are three types of information that a computer model might give in a hurricane forecast?

   _____

   _____

6. 🎯 **Main Idea and Details** Give the main idea of how computer models help scientists forecast hurricanes. Include supporting details.

   _____

   _____

   _____

Name _____

Lesson 2: What are tornadoes?

Vocabulary

tornado a rapidly spinning column of air that comes down out of a
thunderstorm cloud and touches the ground

vortex an area where air or liquid spins, or spirals, in circles

How Tornadoes Form

A **tornado** is a spinning column of air that comes down out of a thunderstorm cloud and touches the ground. An area inside a thunderstorm must be spinning for a tornado to form. This area of spinning air may spin even faster and become a tornado. The winds in a tornado are often less than 200 kilometers per hour, but they can reach speeds of 500 kilometers per hour.

The Vortex

A **vortex** is an area where air or liquid spins in circles. Have you ever watched water go down a drain? A vortex of spinning water may form. A tornado is a vortex that forms in a thunderstorm.

The center of a tornado is made of a low pressure area. A vortex is created when air rushes into this area. A funnel cloud forms inside this vortex. The vortex becomes darker when the funnel cloud picks up dust and other objects. A vortex may be easier to see when it gets darker.

Forecasting Tornadoes

A tornado is difficult to forecast. It can form and move very fast. There is little time to warn people once a tornado is seen.

Meteorologists are scientists who study weather. They use a tool called Doppler radar to look inside a thunderstorm. Doppler radar collects information about wind direction and speed. It can also find the vortex of a tornado and help meteorologists predict tornadoes.

Classifying Tornadoes

A tornado's winds can cause a great deal of damage. Scientists classify tornadoes by their wind speeds and the damage they cause.

Safety

A tornado watch means that a tornado is likely to form within hours. A tornado warning means that a tornado has formed.

You should go into the basement and hide under a table when there is a tornado warning. Find a small room such as a bathroom, closet, or hallway without windows if you are in a building without a basement. Stay away from the outside walls of the building. Lie down in a low area if you are outside, and do not stay in a car.

Comparing Tornadoes and Hurricanes

How are tornadoes and hurricanes alike? Both tornadoes and hurricanes are very strong storms. Both storms spin around a center of low air pressure. Both storms also have high winds that can cause much damage.

How are tornadoes and hurricanes different? A hurricane is much larger than a tornado. It has many thunderstorms. A hurricane forms over an ocean. A hurricane can last many days. A tornado forms in one thunderstorm. It usually forms over land. A tornado lasts only a few minutes. A tornado's winds can be much faster than a hurricane's winds.

© Pearson Education, Inc. 4

Name _____

Lesson 2 Checkpoint

1. What are three ways in which a tornado is different from
   a hurricane?

   _____

   _____

   _____

2. How does Doppler radar help scientists know what is happening
   inside a thunderstorm?

   _____

   _____

3. What are the safest parts of a building when a tornado warning is
   given for your area?

   _____

   _____

4. **Main Idea and Details** Give the main idea of how a tornado
   forms in a thunderstorm. Include supporting details.

   _____

   _____

   _____

   _____

Name _____

Lesson 1: What are minerals?

Vocabulary

minerals natural, nonliving solid crystals that make up rocks

luster the way a mineral's surface reflects light

Mineral Crystals

Salt is a mineral. A metal fork is made of minerals. **Minerals** are natural, nonliving solid crystals that make up rocks.

Each mineral has crystals that are a certain shape. For example, fluorite is a mineral that has cube-shaped crystals. Corundum is another mineral that has crystals with about six sides. All over the world, each mineral is made of the same chemicals. For example, quartz in Australia has the same chemicals as quartz in Arkansas.

There are more than 3,000 minerals. But the rocks in Earth's crust have only about 30 minerals. They are called "rock-forming" minerals. Most rocks are made of different kinds of minerals, but each kind of rock is always made of the same minerals. For example, granite is a type of rock. Granite is always made of quartz and feldspar. A few rocks are made of only one or two minerals. For example, white marble is made only of the mineral calcite.

How to Identify a Mineral

Scientists can identify the minerals in a rock. They test the rock's physical properties. These properties are color, luster, hardness, streak, and cleavage.

A mineral's color is easy to see. Feldspar is a mineral. But it can be pink or white. Scientists cannot identify a mineral just by its color. Scientists also look at a mineral's luster. **Luster** is the way a mineral's surface reflects light. The luster can be dull, metallic, pearly, glassy, greasy, or silky.

Hardness

Scientists also test a mineral's hardness. They find out how easily a mineral can be scratched. They use a chart called the Mohs Scale for Hardness. This chart orders minerals from 1 to 10. A mineral with a higher number can scratch all the minerals with a lower number. For example, the mineral topaz is an 8. Quartz is a 7. Topaz can scratch quartz.

Streak

Another test is a streak test. For this test, a mineral is scratched on a special plate. The mineral leaves a powder. Streak is the color of this powder. A mineral can come in different colors. But its streak is always the same color. For example, halite is a mineral that can have different colors. Halite can be clear or white. It can have yellow, red, or blue bits in it. But halite's streak is always white.

© Pearson Education, Inc. **4**

Lesson 1 Checkpoint

1. What are minerals?

_____

_____

2. 🎯 **Summarize** Each mineral has the same chemical makeup no matter where it is found. Which details support this summary of the second paragraph on page 239 of your textbook?

_____

_____

3. What are rocks made of?

_____

_____

4. Why is the streak test useful?

_____

_____

5. 🎯 **Summarize** What would happen if you scratched a piece of quartz against a piece of hornblende? Look at the chart on page 241 of your textbook to find the answer. Explain your answer.

_____

_____

_____

Lesson 2: How are sedimentary rocks formed?

Vocabulary

sediment eroded material that settles on the bottoms of lakes, rivers, and oceans

sedimentary rock rock that forms over time as sediment becomes cemented together and hardens

Layers of Rock

Erosion is when water, ice, wind, and gravity wear down rock or soil. The tiny pieces of rock settle on the bottoms of lakes, rivers, and oceans. The eroded rock and dirt is called **sediment.** Newer layers of sediment settle on top of older layers, pressing the older layers together. Sticky clay minerals glue the particles together. They become hard and become **sedimentary rock**.

Types of Sedimentary Rock

Limestone is a sedimentary rock made of the bones and shells of sea animals that lived long ago. Sandstone forms from small pieces of quartz, each about the size of a grain of sand. Mudstone is another kind of sedimentary rock that is made in lakes or oceans from tiny pieces of clay minerals.

How Rocks Change into Soil

Over time, loose rocks on Earth's surface wear down. Water drips into cracks in rocks. The water freezes and then thaws, or melts, making the cracks larger and the rock weaker. After a while, the rock breaks apart. Even plant roots can get into a rock and break it. This is called *weathering*.

Soil is made of little pieces of weathered rock. There are also dead plant and animal parts in soil as well as tiny living things, such as bacteria, fungi, worms, and insects. They break plant and animal remains into nutrients for plants to use.

How Stone Tells a Story

Fossils help scientists learn about old plant and animal life on Earth. Many fossils are found in sedimentary rock. Some examples are dinosaur footprints or a copy of teeth from an extinct animal. Bones, shells, teeth, and leaves are also fossils. Dinosaur tracks can show whether a dinosaur walked on two or four legs. Fossils also show that Earth has changed. For example, fossils of giant sea turtles that were found in South Dakota prove that water once covered this area.

How a Fossil Forms

An animal's soft body parts wear away after the animal dies. Its skeleton, teeth, and other hard parts of the body remain. Sediment like sand or mud bury these parts. Minerals from the sediment replace minerals in the body parts. The sediment hardens into rock. After many years, the layers of rock erode. The fossil appears at the surface.

Fossils help scientists learn about Earth's history. They can find out the age of the rock layer the fossil was found in.

Geologic Time Scale

A geologic time scale divides Earth's history into four time periods. The earliest period is at the bottom. Newer periods are at the top. The scale's order is like layers of sedimentary rock. The layers with the oldest fossils are at the bottom. Newer layers of rock form on top.

© Pearson Education, Inc. 4

Lesson 2 Checkpoint

1. How does water freezing and thawing cause weathering?

_____

_____

_____

_____

2. **Summarize** What makes up soil?

_____

_____

_____

3. What kinds of materials end up as sediments?

_____

_____

4. Describe how an organism becomes a fossil.

_____

_____

_____

_____

5. **Summarize** how fossils help scientists.

_____

_____

Lesson 3: What are igneous and metamorphic rocks?

Vocabulary

igneous rocks rocks that form from molten rock

metamorphic rocks rocks that have changed as a result of heat and pressure

Igneous Rocks

Did you know that rocks can melt? Under Earth's crust is a layer of rock. It is so hot that it is partly melted. This rock is called magma. **Igneous rocks** form from this molten rock.

Igneous rocks can form above or below Earth's surface. Magma is thrown onto the Earth's surface when a volcano erupts. Magma is called lava after it reaches the surface. Lava cools quickly. It hardens into igneous rock. This can happen in a few days. An igneous rock that cools quickly has no time to form crystals.

Most igneous rocks are not made this way. Instead, magma rises to the Earth's surface. It slowly fills spaces in the crust. The magma changes into igneous rock. Mineral crystals form in this rock. This very slow process can take more than a million years!

The Giant's Causeway

A causeway is a road that is built above water. Pillars hold up the road. About 40,000 of these columns are near the coast of Northern Ireland. The tops of the posts form a path to the sea. They are called the Giant's Causeway.

How did the posts form? Between 50 to 60 million years ago, lava cooled quickly when it reached the sea. The lava became squeezed together as it cooled and turned into rock. The rock cracked from top to bottom and formed the huge pillars.

Metamorphic Rocks

The temperature below Earth's crust can melt rock. Rock is also under a lot of pressure. Rocks that change because of this heat and pressure are called **metamorphic rocks.**

Metamorphic rocks can form from sedimentary or igneous rock. Metamorphic rock can change in many ways. Heat and pressure may change the mineral crystals in a rock. The shape and size of a rock's mineral crystals can change. Chemicals in the rock may also form new minerals.

The Rock Cycle

Old rocks are always changing into new rocks. This process is called the rock cycle. Heat, pressure, weathering, and erosion are some forces of this cycle. Not all rocks complete the cycle. Some rocks may only go through part of the cycle.

© Pearson Education, Inc. **4**

Lesson 3 Checkpoint

1. Which igneous rock will have larger crystals, one that cooled slowly or one that cooled quickly?

   _____

   _____

2. Compare and contrast the two ways igneous rock can form.

   _____

   _____

   _____

   _____

3. What causes sedimentary or igneous rock to turn into metamorphic rock?

   _____

   _____

Lesson 1: How does Earth's surface wear away?

Vocabulary

landform a natural feature on Earth's surface such as mountains, hills, valleys, plains, plateaus, and coastal features

weathering process in which rocks in Earth's crust are slowly broken into smaller pieces. This is done by either chemical or physical weathering.

Earth's Crust

A layer of rock covers Earth. This layer is called the crust. A mountain is one shape of Earth's crust. A mountain is a landform. The Earth's crust has many **landforms** of different sizes and shapes. Plains are flat landforms. They are on low ground. Plateaus are flat landforms on high ground. Peninsulas, valleys, and canyons are also landforms.

How Weathering Affects Landforms

Water, ice, temperature changes, chemicals, and living things cause Earth's crust to slowly wear away. This is called **weathering**. There are two kinds of weathering. There is physical weathering and chemical weathering.

Physical Weathering

Physical weathering changes the size of rocks. Large rocks break into smaller pieces. These pieces are all made of the same kind of rock. Water is one cause of physical weathering. Moving water carries small pieces of rock, soil, and sand. The pieces rub against each other. They slowly get smaller.

Ice also causes physical weathering. Water fills the cracks in rocks. Then, the water freezes and turns into ice. Ice takes up more space than water. This cracks the rock. The cracks get larger every time this happens. Finally, the rock can break.

Changes in a rock's temperature cause physical weathering. A rock grows larger when it gets hot. A rock gets smaller when it gets cold. These changes weaken the outside of the rock.

Living things can cause physical weathering, too. Have you seen a plant growing from a crack in the sidewalk? Plants can also grow in cracks in rocks. The plant's roots break the rock.

Chemical Weathering

Chemical weathering causes rock to break, but it changes the material that makes up a rock. For example, rainwater mixes with carbon dioxide in the air. This makes an acid that joins with rock material when it rains. This makes a new chemical. Slowly, the new chemical breaks the rock into smaller pieces.

Animals and plants also give off chemicals that cause weathering. Sometimes, people's activities can also add chemicals to the environment.

Lesson 1 Checkpoint

1. List five examples of landforms.

_____

_____

_____

2. List 4 causes of weathering.

_____

_____

_____

3. Why do cracks in a rock get larger because water has frozen in them?

_____

_____

_____

4. **Compare and Contrast** How are physical weathering and chemical weathering alike? How are they different?

_____

_____

_____

Lesson 2: How do weathered materials move?

Vocabulary

erosion the movement of weathered pieces of rock by water, ice, and wind

deposition the laying down of pieces of Earth's surface

landslide a rapid downhill movement of a large amount of rock and soil

Effects of Erosion

Water, ice, gravity, and wind move weathered pieces of rock. This movement is called **erosion.**

Water carries material away from landforms and rocks. Rain carries this material to streams. Streams can carry the material a long way. Water moving downhill very slowly wears away rocks and soil that form canyons and valleys.

Waves change the shape of a shoreline. Waves carry pieces of sand away from the shore. Waves hit cracks in rocks on the shore. Slowly, pieces of rock break off and are carried away by waves. The shoreline erodes, forming new beaches.

Glaciers also wear away landforms. Glaciers are huge sheets of ice that move very slowly. Glaciers also rip rocks apart. Like running water, glaciers carry rock far away.

Deposition

Moving water or wind carries rock and soil from one place to another. Pieces of rock and soil laid down on Earth's surface become **deposition.**

As moving water slows, larger rocks settle to the bottom first. Then smaller pieces sink. The smallest pieces of soil are called silt. Pieces of silt are the last to sink. Rivers drop large amounts of material where they flow into an ocean. The material forms a fan-shaped area called a delta.

Wind also causes deposition. Wind carries silt and drops it onto the ground. The silt forms a layer on top of the soil.

Gravity and Landslides

Earth's gravity pulls matter from higher places to lower places. Heavy rains or earthquakes can loosen material on a hill. Gravity pulls this rock and soil downward. This is called a **landslide.** Landslides are different from other kinds of erosion and deposition. They move a lot of material quickly.

Gravity and Avalanches

Gravity can also pull large amounts of snow and ice downhill. This is called an avalanche. Strong winds, earthquakes, and explosions can cause avalanches. People try to prevent avalanches by clearing away large amounts of snow.

Controlling Erosion and Deposition

Erosion and deposition happen when land does not have trees or plants to stop wind and water from eroding the rocks and soil.

Erosion can be controlled by growing plants. The plants' roots hold the soil in place. Leaves can stop some rain from washing away soil. Farmers can plow hilly fields in steps. These steps are called terraces. Terraces keep rainwater from running downhill. People can also build walls on the seashore to keep large waves from carrying sand away.

Sometimes people want to limit deposition. For example, they may dig soil out of waterways to help ships pass.

© Pearson Education, Inc. 4

Quick Study

Name _____

Lesson 2 Checkpoint

1. Which particles are the first to settle as moving water slows?

_____

_____

2. List three things that cause both erosion and deposition.

_____

_____

_____

3. How is a landslide different from other kinds of erosion and deposition?

_____

_____

_____

4. **Compare and Contrast** erosion and deposition caused by running water with erosion and deposition caused by a glacier.

_____

_____

_____

Name _____

Lesson 3: How can Earth's surface change rapidly?

Vocabulary

volcano a cone-shaped landform at a weak spot in Earth's crust where magma reaches the surface

fault a break or crack in rock where Earth's crust can move

earthquake a shaking of Earth's crust caused by sudden movements at a fault

epicenter the point on Earth's surface that is directly above the focus of an earthquake

Volcanoes

A **volcano** is a cone-shaped landform that forms at weak spots in Earth's crust. Volcanoes can quickly change Earth's surface.

Before a volcano forms, underground hot rock, called magma, is partly melted into liquid. Gases in the magma push it upwards. A volcano erupts when magma reaches its surface. Magma is called lava when it flows out of the volcano. Sometimes, it explodes out of the volcano. Other times, magma slowly oozes out of the volcano. The temperature and the kind of rock in the magma control the kind of eruption.

Volcanic eruptions can create rock and ash. Ash flew more than 15 miles into the air when Mount St. Helens erupted. It covered land and cities near the volcano, killing trees and animals.

Active and Dormant Volcanoes

Active volcanoes erupt often or show signs of erupting such as Kilauea in Hawaii. Dormant volcanoes have not erupted for a long time. Mount Rainer in Washington has not had a major eruption in over 500 years.

A volcano is extinct if no eruptions have been recorded. Mount Kenya in Africa is an extinct volcano.

Earth's Moving Plates

The Earth's outer layer is the crust. It rests on another layer called the upper mantle. These layers are divided into large pieces called plates. Plates always move. Most volcanoes are near places where plates come together.

The Cause of Earthquakes

A **fault** is a break in rock where Earth's crust can move. Rocks near a fault can get stuck but the plates keep moving. This puts pressure on the rocks. This pressure can break the rocks, and can also cause plates to move. This is an **earthquake.**

The place underground where the plates start to move is called the focus. This is where the earthquake begins. The point on Earth's surface right above the focus is the **epicenter**.

Plates give off energy as they move along a fault. This energy moves away from the focus in all directions. It causes greatest damage near the epicenter.

Effects of Earthquakes and Volcanoes

Mount Tambora in Asia erupted in 1815. The volcano's ash filled the sky. Less sunlight could reach Earth. This caused snow to fall in the northeastern United States in June.

In 1906, strong earthquakes broke power lines in San Francisco and caused fires that burned for three days and destroyed 500 city blocks.

Quick Study

© Pearson Education, Inc. 4

Lesson 3 Checkpoint

1. What causes magma to rise to the surface beneath a volcano?

_____

_____

2. Why are some volcanic eruptions more powerful than others?

_____

_____

3. Explain how the actions around a fault can result in an earthquake.

_____

_____

Lesson 1: What are natural resources?

Vocabulary

solar energy the energy given off by the Sun

humus decaying plant and animal remains in soil

How Resources Are Used

Natural resources are materials from nature. Plants and animals are natural resources. Nonliving things, such as air, water, soil, minerals, and sunlight are also natural resources. All living things need natural resources. We use natural resources to make the things we eat, use, or buy.

Renewable Natural Resources

There are renewable and nonrenewable resources. Renewable resources can be replaced. **Solar energy** is energy from the sun. It is renewable. Water, oxygen, trees, and soil are also renewable resources. Soil, which covers most of the land on Earth, is a renewable resource. Many animals make their homes in soil. Trees and other plants need soil to live. It is a nonliving natural resource.

How Soil Is Renewed

Weathering, erosion, and deposition form soil. Water and wind break rocks into small pieces. This is weathering. Water, ice, or wind moves the weathered pieces of rock. This is erosion. The weathered pieces are left in different places. This is deposition.

Ingredients in Soil

Bits of weathered rock are a main part of soil. Decaying plant and animal matter called **humus**, air, and minerals are also part of soil. Tiny organisms such as fungi, bacteria, worms, and insects live in soil. They break down plant and animal matter into nutrients. Plants use these nutrients as food.

Different soils form from different kinds of rocks and minerals. The amount of humus in soil affects how it feels. Minerals in the soil may affect its color. Soil samples from places that are only a few kilometers apart can look and feel very different!

Clay, Salt, and Sand

Clay soil is made of the smallest particles. Clay may be different colors because of the materials in it. For example, clay with iron particles looks red. Some clay feels sticky.

Silt is another kind of soil. Particles in silt are larger than particles in clay. Silt particles feel smooth. The largest particles form sand. Sand has different materials in it. Quartz is the most common mineral in sand. Broken shells are in sand that is near oceans. Some sand is very light colored but other sand is very dark depending on what is in it.

Soil for Growing Plants

Plants grow well in soil with many nutrients. If the soil has too much sand or clay, plants cannot get nutrients from the soil. A good soil for plants has the right mix of clay, sand, and humus.

Soil as a Renewable Natural Resource

Soil is renewable. Farmers can plant crops that put nutrients back into the soil. But soil takes a long time to replace. Only a few centimeters of topsoil are renewed every 1,000 years. Conserving soil is important.

Other Uses of Soil

Soil is used as clay to make tile, bricks, and pottery. Clay is also used to make paper stronger. Concrete and glass are made from sand.

Lesson 1 Checkpoint

1. What are three natural resources?

_____

_____

2. What are three key ingredients in soil?

_____

_____

_____

3. Soil is a renewable resource. What keeps it from renewing easily?

_____

_____

4. **Cause and Effect** How do the amounts of sand, silt, and clay in soil affect plant growth?

_____

_____

Name _____

Lesson 2: How are resources used for energy?

Vocabulary

solar cell a device that changes energy from the Sun into electrical energy

ore a mineral-rich rock that can be removed from Earth

fossil fuels made from the remains of organisms that lived long ago

petroleum an oil that is a fossil fuel; a nonrenewable energy source

conservation using only what you need as efficiently as possible

recycling saving, collecting, or using materials again

Renewable Energy Sources

The sun, wind, and moving water create renewable energy. Plants need sunlight to make food. Solar energy is energy from the Sun. Solar energy is renewable. It also creates wind energy and water energy.

How We Use Solar Energy

A **solar cell** changes energy from the Sun into electrical energy. Solar energy can give power to big jobs. Solar panels are used to collect the Sun's energy to be changed into electric energy or heat energy.

Wind energy, which has been used for years, is also renewable. Windmills run machines, pump water, and produce electric power.

Energy from Flowing Water

Moving water has energy. It is used to power machines that produce electricity. Dams control the flow of water. Water is kept in a lake behind the dam and the water is released when its energy is needed.

Nonrenewable Energy Sources

Nonrenewable resources cannot be replaced. Nonrenewable resources are used to make products and provide energy. **Ore** is a mineral-rich rock that is used to make products.

Fossil Fuels

Coal, natural gas, and **petroleum** are nonrenewable resources. These **fossil fuels** are burned to make heat. They are made from organisms that lived long ago.

Mining fossil fuels can harm the environment. Some of the richest oil is under the ocean floor. An oil spill is one of the biggest dangers of drilling under the ocean. Spills can cause pollution and also kill or hurt plants and animals. Using fossil fuels can also have harmful effects. Burning fossil fuels releases smoke, ash, and gases into the air, making the air unhealthy to breathe. Carbon dioxide gas can lead to global warming.

Energy Conservation

Conservation helps our resources last longer. There are many ways to conserve energy such as walking instead of riding in a car. Turn off water and lights you are not using. You can use machines that use less energy.

Recycling

Recycling is saving, collecting, or using things again instead of throwing them away. Many recycled products are made from glass, cardboard, paper, tin, steel, glass, and some plastics.

© Pearson Education, Inc. 4

Lesson 2 Checkpoint

1. How do we capture and use solar energy?

_____

_____

2. How are Earth's resources reduced?

_____

_____

3. **Cause and Effect** What are some harmful results from using fossil fuels?

_____

_____

_____

_____

4. How can we conserve energy?

_____

_____

_____

_____

Use with pp. 319–321

Lesson 1: What is matter?

Properties of Matter

All living and nonliving things are made of matter. Matter is anything that has mass and takes up space. You can describe matter. You can use your senses to identify properties of matter. Some properties of matter are color, size, and shape.

Testing Matter

Choose an object to describe. Look at the object to see what color, size, or shape it is. Touch the object to find out if it is rough or smooth, or hot or cold. See what happens if you heat or cool it. Use a magnet to see if the object is attracted to it. Move the object to find out if it is flexible. Does it bend or does it break? Put the object in water. Does it float? Does it change?

States of Matter

Matter is made up of tiny particles. These particles are too small to see. The tiny particles of matter move. The particles are arranged in different ways. The state of matter depends on how the particles move and the way they are arranged. The three most common states of matter are solids, liquids, and gases. Most substances on Earth can be found in only one natural state. Water is found in nature in all three states. The state of water depends on the temperature. Water is a liquid. When it gets cold it freezes into ice. Ice is a solid. When water is heated, it evaporates. It becomes water vapor, which is a gas.

Solids

An ice cube is the same shape when it is on a plate or in a glass. It is a solid. A solid has a definite shape and takes up a definite amount of space. The particles are close together. They move back and forth but do not change places with each other.

Liquids

Water takes the same shape as the container it fills. It is a liquid. A liquid does not have a definite shape, but it takes up a definite amount of space. The particles are not held together as tightly as in a solid. The particles can slide past one another.

Gases

Water vapor is part of the air we breathe. It is a gas. Like a liquid, water vapor takes the same shape of the container it fills and has no definite shape. A gas always expands to fill whatever space is available. The particles move far apart from one another and move in all directions. Particles in a gas move around more easily and quickly than particles in a solid.

Lesson 1 Checkpoint

1. Group five different objects in your classroom by properties. Describe the properties.

_____

_____

_____

_____

_____

2. Name the solid and gas forms of water.

_____

_____

3. Draw a diagram to show the arrangement and movement of particles for one state of matter.

_____

4. ⟳ **Compare and contrast** the movement of particles in solids, liquids, and gases.

_____

_____

_____

Lesson 2: How is matter measured?

Vocabulary

density the amount of mass in a certain volume of matter

Mass

Mass is the measure of the amount of matter in an object. Your mass is the same wherever you go. The mass of an object does not change unless we add matter to it or remove matter from it.

Using a Pan Balance

You can use a pan balance to find the mass of an object. Suppose that you measure the mass of a toy. It is 23 grams. Then if you take it apart and measure its mass, it will still be 23 grams. If someone else takes all the parts of the toy and makes a toy that looks very different, the mass will still be the same. The only way to change the toy's mass is to add parts or not use all the parts.

Metric Units of Mass

Scientists use metric units to measure and compare matter. Some metric units are: gram (g), milligram (mg), and kilogram (kg). One kilogram is 1,000 grams. One gram is 1,000 milligrams.

Volume

Volume is the amount of space that matter takes up. Like mass, volume can be measured. You can measure the volume of something solid, like a box, by counting the number of cubes that fill it. Or you can measure the length, width, and height of the box and multiply these three measurements. If a box is 5 cm long, 2 cm wide, and 8 cm high, then its volume is 5 cm x 2 cm x 8 cm, or 80 cubic cm. Some metric units scientists use to measure volume of solids are cubic centimeters (cm^3) and cubic meters (m^3).

Volume of Liquids

To measure the volume of a liquid, you need to put it in a measuring container, such as a graduated cylinder. The units on a graduated cylinder are milliliters (mL) and liters (L). A liter is equal to 1,000 milliliters.

Volume of Other Objects

You can also use a graduated cylinder to measure the volume of solids that sink in water, such as a ball. Put water in the cylinder. Measure the water. Then add the ball and measure how many milliliters the water rises. This is the volume of the ball.

Density

The amount of mass in a certain volume of matter is a property called **density**. Suppose you have a piece of wood and a piece of steel that are the same size. If the steel has more mass than the wood, the steel has greater density than the wood.

Finding Density

You find an object's density by dividing its mass by its volume. The units to measure density are grams per cubic centimeter. You write density as a fraction: g/cm^3. An object's density tells whether it will float or sink in a liquid. For example, water floats on top of oil because water's density is less than oil's. But the density of a cork is less than the density of water, so the cork floats.

Lesson 2 Checkpoint

1. Explain why your mass is the same wherever you go.

_____

_____

2. What metric units are used to measure the volume of solids? Of liquids?

_____

_____

3. Explain why steel sinks in water and cork floats.

_____

_____

4. An unpeeled orange floats in water, but a peeled orange sinks. What can you conclude about the density of an unpeeled orange?

_____

_____

Name _____

Lesson 3: How do substances mix?

Vocabulary

mixture a combination of two or more substances that keep their individual properties

solution a combination of two or more substances where one is dissolved by the other

solute the substance that is dissolved in a solution

solvent the substance that dissolves another substance in a solution

solubility the ability of one substance to dissolve in another

Mixtures

A **mixture** is a combination of two or more substances. You can separate substances in a mixture easily. For example, we can make a vegetable mixture of peas, carrots, and corn. You can sort out each vegetable into a separate pile. Each vegetable tastes the same whether it is separate or not. All substances in a mixture can be separated. They have the same properties as they did before they were mixed.

You can separate mixtures in different ways. In a mixture of beads, sand, and safety pins, you can separate the pins with a magnet. Then you can put the sand and beads in water so that the beads float to the top.

Solutions

If you stir salt and water together, you can make a mixture. The salt will dissolve in the water, so you cannot see it. This kind of mixture is called a **solution.** In a solution, one or more substances are dissolved in another substance. The most common kind of solution is a solid such as salt dissolved in a liquid.

In a solution made of a liquid and a solid, the substance that is dissolved is the **solute.** In a solution of salt and water, the salt is the solute. A **solvent**
is the substance that dissolves the other substance. In a salt and water solution, the solvent is water. Usually there is more of the solvent than the other substance.

Common Solutions

Ocean water is a solution that contains salt and other minerals. But a solution does not have to be a liquid. For example, the air we breathe is a solution made of gases. A solution can also be a solid. For example, steel is a solution made from carbon and iron.

Solubility

Solubility is a measurement of how much of a substance will dissolve in another substance. For example, sand will not dissolve in water, so the solubility of sand in water is zero. Sometimes you can increase the solubility of a substance by increasing the temperature. For example, you can dissolve more sugar in warm water than you can in cold water.

Another way to make a solute dissolve quicker is to crush it. If you drop a sugar cube into a cup of water, it may take a long time to dissolve. But if you crush the sugar cube into tiny crystals, it will dissolve very quickly. This is because more of the sugar touches the water when it is in tiny crystals than when it is in a cube.

© Pearson Education, Inc. 4

Lesson 3 Checkpoint

1. When the bead, sand, and salt mixture pictured on pages 328–329 of your textbook is put into water, the yellow beads float. What does this tell you about the density of a yellow bead?

   _____

   _____

2. What are the parts of a solution?

   _____

   _____

3. What factors affect the solubility of a substance?

   _____

   _____

   _____

Lesson 4: How does matter change?

Vocabulary

physical change a change in the size, shape, or state of matter

chemical change a change that that results in a new substance

Physical Changes

If you cut and fold a piece of paper, you change only the size and shape of the paper. You do not change the particles that make up the paper. A change in the size, shape, or state of matter is a **physical change.** The particles that make up the matter stay the same.

Breaking a pencil is a physical change. Another physical change is tearing. If you tear a sheet of paper into a hundred pieces, it is still made of the same kind of matter. If you make a bowl out of a piece of clay, the bowl is still the same piece of clay. It has the same properties, but it is a different shape. It has only changed physically.

When you make a mixture, you create a physical change. It is a physical change because the particles in the mixture do not change. They can be separated.

Phase Changes

If you freeze water into an ice cube and then let it melt, the liquid is still water. Ice and water are the same substance in different states. These states are called phases. Phase changes are a kind of physical change. A mass of a substance does not change when it changes phases.

Substances can change phase if you add or take away energy. For example, you put water into a freezer to cool it and make ice. You add energy to water when you heat it. If you boil water in a pot, some of it becomes water vapor, or steam.

Every substance changes phases at a different temperature. The temperature at which a solid changes to a liquid is called the melting point. The boiling point of a material is the temperature at which it changes from a liquid, such as water, to a gas, such as water vapor.

Chemical Changes

Unlike physical change, a **chemical change** makes a completely different kind of matter. In a chemical change, a substance is changed in some way to make a new substance with different properties. For example, if you leave an iron nail in a damp place, it will rust. Rust and iron have different properties. The color and hardness of rust and iron are different.

Elements

The simplest pure substances are called elements. There are more than 100 elements. Scientists have organized information about these elements in a chart. This chart is called the Periodic Table.

Lesson 4 Checkpoint

1. Sawing wood, shredding paper, and crushing a sugar cube are physical changes. Give examples of three other actions that are physical changes.

   _____

   _____

   _____

2. How does adding or taking away heat energy cause changes in matter?

   _____

   _____

3. What is a chemical change?

   _____

   _____

4. When you chew food, are you causing physical or chemical changes to the food?

   _____

5. 🎯 **Compare and Contrast** How are rusting and burning different? How are they alike?

   _____

   _____

Lesson 1: Why does matter have energy?

Vocabulary

thermal energy energy due to moving particles that make up matter

Energy in Matter

Rub your hands together. What happens? Your hands became warmer. You used energy to make heat. Energy is the ability to change something or do work. All changes need energy.

All matter is made of tiny, moving particles. The particles in a solid are very close together. They move a little bit. The particles in a liquid are close together but they can move past each other. The particles in a gas are far apart and move in many directions.

An object's particles move faster as the object becomes hotter. An object's particles move more slowly as the object becomes cooler. Moving particles make **thermal energy.** We feel thermal energy as heat. You felt thermal energy when you rubbed your hands together.

Measuring Moving Particles

A thermometer is a tool that is used to measure temperature. Most thermometers are thin glass tubes that are connected to a bulb. The bulb holds colored alcohol. The lines on the outside of the thin tube show degrees.

A thermometer's bulb is placed on or in the matter being measured. The matter may have particles that are moving very

fast. This makes the liquid particles inside the thermometer speed up too. The liquid particles move farther apart. This causes the liquid to move up the tube. The reading on the number line shows a greater number of degrees. The liquid particles move closer together when the matter's particles slow down. This causes the liquid to move down the tube. The reading on the number line will show a lesser number of degrees.

Heat and Temperature

Many of us confuse the meanings of the words *heat* and *temperature*. The difference between the two is the movement of particles in matter. Temperature measures the average energy of the matter. Thermal energy measures the total energy of the moving particles. It measures how fast the particles move and how many particles are moving. Heat is the transfer of thermal energy from one piece of matter to another.

Think of a large pot and a small pot of boiling water. The larger pot took longer to boil because it holds more water particles than the small pot. The large pot also has more thermal energy. The temperature of both pots is the same. This means the average motion of the particles in the water is also the same.

Lesson 1 Checkpoint

1. What is energy?

_____

_____

2. Explain why a large pot of water takes longer to begin boiling than a small pot. Both pots started with the same temperature of water, and burners for both pots are set on "high."

_____

_____

_____

_____

3. **Cause and Effect** What causes liquid in a thermometer to travel up and down the tube?

_____

_____

_____

_____

Lesson 2: How does heat move?

Vocabulary

---

conduction the transfer of heat energy by one thing touching another

conductor a material that readily allows heat to move

insulator a material that limits the amount of heat that passes through it

convection current a pattern of flowing heat energy; formed when heated fluid expands

radiation energy that is sent out without particles

Conduction

Thermal energy always moves from warmer areas to cooler ones. Heat is thermal energy that moves between matters with different temperatures. It can be moved by conduction. **Conduction** is the transfer of heat energy by one thing touching another.

Conductors and Insulators

A **conductor** is a material that allows heat to move easily. Many metals, such as aluminum, copper, and iron are good conductors.

An **insulator** is a material that limits the amount of heat that passes through it. Have you ever used a wooden spoon to stir hot soup? The wooden spoon does not get warm, as a metal spoon does. Wood, marble, air, and plastic are all good insulators.

Convection

Convection is another way heat moves between matter. It causes a kitchen to get warm when a stove is on. In convection, a fluid moves from place to place. A fluid is a substance that flows. It has no shape. Water is a fluid.

A **convection current** forms when a heated fluid, such as air, expands. A convection current is a pattern of flowing heat energy. It becomes less dense than

the cooler air around it. The cooler air sinks below the warmer air. The warm air is forced upwards. Then the cooler air warms and is forced upward. This pattern continues.

Radiation

Radiation is energy that is sent out in little bundles of energy. Radiation can move energy great distances, like from the Sun to the Earth.

Radiation is different from conduction or convection. Conduction needs particles in matter to crash. Convection needs a fluid to spread when particles crash. Radiation does not need particles. It happens all by itself. Radiation can travel through empty space or through matter.

Conduction, Convection, and Radiation

Earth's surface heats up when the Sun's energy reaches Earth. Then conduction takes place. Earth's surface transfers heat to the air. Convection currents form as the air is heated by Earth's surface. That warm air expands and rises. The rising air cools. The water vapor in this air condenses. It falls to Earth as rain or snow. Convection currents in the air cause Earth's wind and rain patterns.

© Pearson Education, Inc. 4

Lesson 2 Checkpoint

1. What is the difference between an insulator and a conductor?

_____

_____

2. How does a convection current form?

_____

_____

_____

_____

3. How does energy from the Sun reach Earth?

_____

_____

4. **Cause and Effect** What causes Earth's surface to get warm?

_____

_____

_____

Lesson 1: How does matter become charged?

Vocabulary

static electricity an imbalance of positive or negative charges

Electric Charges

Atoms are the tiny building blocks of matter. Most atoms have three different particles. Some particles have a positive charge (+). Some particles have a negative charge (–). Some particles have no charge. Matter usually has the same number of positive particles as negative particles. This makes the matter neutral.

Charged particles can move between objects that are close to each other. **Static electricity** is the result when positive and negative charges no longer balance. Static electricity may move slowly or quickly. Moving charges make electrical energy. This energy changes into sound, light, and heat energy.

Static Electricity

In storm clouds, charged particles move between atoms. This causes the clouds to become charged. Often, the positive particles move near the top of clouds. The negative particles move near the bottom of clouds. This static electricity is released as lightning. It heats up the nearby air and makes the air glow. Lightning also creates thunder.

How Charged Objects Behave

You can predict how charged objects will act. Pretend two objects have opposite charges. One is positive. The other is negative. The objects will pull toward each other. This is an electric force. An electric force is the push or pull between objects that have different charges.

A charged object can attract something that has no charge. What happens if you rub a balloon on your hair? The balloon picks up negative particles from your hair. It becomes negatively charged. What happens if you hold the balloon near a light, neutral object? The balloon will stick to the object. For example, a charged balloon will stick to a wall. After awhile, the balloon loses its negative charge. It falls off the wall.

Two objects that have the same charge push away from each other, or repel. What happens when you put a hat on your head in the winter? Negative particles move from your hair to the hat. Your hair becomes positively charged. What happens when you take the hat off? All the positively charged hairs stand up. They move away from other positively charged hairs. Two objects that have the same charge push away from one another.

An Electric Field

The space around electrically charged objects is called an electric field. We cannot see an electric field. It is strongest when it is close to the charged object. The electric field gets weaker farther from the object.

An electric field causes an electric force on charged objects that touch it. A positive electric field attracts negative charges. It pushes away positive charges. A negative electric field attracts positive charges. It pushes away negative charges.

Name _____

Lesson 1 Checkpoint

1. What causes static electricity on an object?

_____

_____

2. What effect will a charged object have on an object with the opposite charge?

_____

_____

3. Give two examples of static electricity.

_____

_____

_____

Use with pp. 378–381

Lesson 2: How do electric charges flow?

Vocabulary

electric current an electric charge in motion

resistance a quality of a material that does not allow electric charge to easily flow through it

series circuit a simple circuit in which an electric charge can only flow in one path

parallel circuit has two or more paths in which an electric charge can flow

How Electric Charges Move

Static electricity stays in one place. Most electricity moves. An electric charge that moves is called an **electric current.** It moves from one place to another so quickly, you cannot see it.

A circuit is a loop that cannot have any breaks in order for electric charges to move through it. It must be a closed circuit. An open circuit has at least one break in it. This stops the flow of electric charges.

Going with the Flow

Electric current does not move the same way in all materials. Some atoms become more easily charged than others. These atoms make up materials called conductors. Most metals are good conductors.

Other materials are made of atoms that do not become charged easily. These materials are called insulators. Electric current moves through them more slowly.

A Closed Circuit

Look at the parts of a closed circuit on page 379 in your textbook.

- **Energy source** power that makes the electric charge flow
- **Means of Energy Transfer** the path through which the electric charge flows
- **Resistor** A coiled wire inside the light bulb made of a material with high resistance. **Resistance** means the

material does not let electric current flow easily through it. This causes the wire to build up electric energy that is given off as heat and light.

- **Insulated Wire** copper wire is insulated with plastic prevents electrical charges from touching other wires.
- **Switch** The circuit is closed when the switch is closed. Electric charge can flow without stopping.

Types of Circuits

The electrical charges in a **series circuit** can only move in one path. The charged particles flow in one direction around a loop. All the bulbs share the electric current equally. None of the bulbs will be brighter than the others. If a bulb burns out, it acts like an "off" switch and opens the circuit. The other bulbs will not get the energy they need and will not light.

Parallel Circuits

A **parallel circuit** has two or more paths for the electric charge to follow. How charges flow on one path does not affect how charges flow on another path.

Circuits in your home and school are parallel circuits. Unlike a series circuit, a break in one part does not stop the charge from flowing. Other bulbs will stay lit even if one bulb burns out. A parallel circuit can also support electrical objects that need different amounts of current.

© Pearson Education, Inc. 4

Lesson 2 Checkpoint

1. What is the difference between an insulator and a conductor?

_____

_____

2. 🎯 **Cause and Effect** What causes some materials to be good insulators of electricity?

_____

_____

3. What is the main difference between a series circuit and a parallel circuit?

_____

_____

4. Why are most homes wired in a parallel circuit rather than a series circuit?

_____

_____

Lesson 3: What are magnetic fields?

Vocabulary

magnetism force that pushes or pulls magnetic materials that are near a magnet

magnetic field the invisible field around a magnet

Magnetism

A magnet is anything that attracts other things made of iron, steel, and certain other metals. **Magnetism** is the name of the force that pushes or pulls magnetic materials near a magnet.

Magnetic Fields

Do you know that magnets have fields around them that you cannot see? The **magnetic field** goes out in all directions. The shape of a magnetic field depends on the shape of the magnet. The magnetic field is always strongest at the magnet's ends, or poles.

Magnetic Poles

All magnets have two poles. One pole is north-seeking. The other pole is south-seeking. Opposite poles have opposite charges. Unlike charges are attracted to each other. Like charges push away from each other.

What happens if you break a magnet into two pieces? You will have two magnets, each with its own north-seeking pole and south-seeking pole. A magnet cannot have one pole without the other.

The Largest Magnet in the World

Why does a compass needle always move to the north-south direction? This happens because Earth behaves like a large magnet. Like all magnets, its magnetic field is strongest at the poles. But Earth's magnetic poles are not same as the poles you see on a map. The magnetic north pole is about 1,000 miles away from the North Pole on the map. The magnetic south pole is near the center of Antarctica.

No one knows exactly why Earth acts like a magnet. Some scientists suggest that Earth's outer core is made of hot melted iron. This liquid iron flows around and around as Earth rotates, creating a magnetic field.

How Compasses Work

A compass needle will always point in a north-south direction. This makes it easy to find east and west.

A compass must have a lightweight needle in order for the compass to work properly. Also, the needle must be able to move easily. The compass cannot be close to a magnet. If it is, the needle will point to the magnet. It will no longer point to Earth's magnetic field.

The Northern Lights

There is another way Earth acts like a magnet. Sometimes, we can see lights in the sky called the Aurora Borealis, or Northern Lights. Auroras are caused by charged particles moving quickly from the Sun. The charged particles are attracted to the Earth's magnetic north and south poles. The particles collide with gases in Earth's atmosphere. Atoms in the gases give off light.

Quick Study

Lesson 3 Checkpoint

1. If you break a magnet into two pieces, what happens to its magnetic poles?

   _____

   _____

2. What are some ways that the Earth is like a magnet?

   _____

   _____

   _____

3. Why does a compass needle point in a north-south direction?

   _____

   _____

Lesson 4: How is electricity transformed to magnetism?

Vocabulary

electromagnet a coil of wire wrapped around an iron core that can transform electrical energy into magnetic energy

Electromagnets

In the 1800s, a scientist named Hans Christian Oersted was showing how electric current moved through a wire. A compass sat near the wire. Oersted saw the magnetic needle on the compass move when he turned on the current. The electric current caused a magnetic field. This discovery led to the invention of the electromagnet.

An **electromagnet** is a coil of wire wrapped around an iron core. A current moves through the wire. This creates a magnetic field that surrounds the electromagnet. The wire loses its magnetic power when the current stops. An electromagnet creates a powerful magnet by changing electrical energy into magnetic energy.

Ways to Make the Magnet Stronger

Like other magnets, an electromagnet has a north pole and a south pole. An electromagnet is different from other magnets because you can change its strength. There are three ways to make an electromagnet stronger. One way is to increase the amount of electric current in the wire. You could also increase the number of turns the metal coil has. Finally, you could make the magnetic core larger.

Uses for Electromagnets

Electromagnets are used in many ways. Electromagnets can be used to lift very heavy objects. Electromagnets are also in machines that doctors and scientists use everyday.

Televisions, DVD players, computers, and VCRs all work because of electromagnets. Electromagnets are used to help change electric energy to magnetic energy to mechanical energy.

How a Doorbell Works

Look at the picture of the doorbell on page 388 in your textbook. Pressing the doorbell's button closes the electrical circuit. Electrical current moves to the transformer. This controls how much current is sent to the electromagnet. This electricity magnetizes the electromagnet. The electromagnet pulls up the contact arm. The arm is attached to a piece of metal that hits the bell. This is what makes the sound.

© Pearson Education, Inc. 4

Quick Study

Lesson 4 Checkpoint

1. How is an electromagnet different from a magnet?

_____

_____

2. 🎯 **Cause and Effect** How did noticing cause and effect lead to Hans Christian Oersted's discovery?

_____

_____

_____

3. Why are electromagnets used in many electronic devices?

_____

_____

Lesson 5: How is magnetism transformed to electricity?

Electrical Energy

Today, magnetism is used in many ways to create electricity. Moving a magnet inside a coiled wire creates electricity. Spinning a coiled wire around a magnet also creates electricity.

Pretend you move a magnet. Its magnetic field moves with it. Changing a magnetic field creates electricity. A magnet that is moved quickly makes a strong electric current. A magnet that is moved slowly makes a weak current. The number of coiled loops also changes the strength of the current. More loops means the magnet creates a stronger current.

A Flashlight Without Batteries

Look at page 392 in your textbook. This timeline lists discoveries people have made in using electrical energy. Look for Michael Faraday on the timeline. Faraday was a scientist who invented a machine called the dynamo in 1831. The machine used magnets to change motion into electric current. Faraday made electrical energy by turning a crank. Today, this technology is used in an emergency flashlight. It does not use batteries. Instead, the flashlight produces electricity when you squeeze its handle.

Currents Currently

A generator is a machine that makes electric energy by turning coils of wire around powerful magnets. Generators used in homes, schools, and businesses are much bigger than those used by Faraday. But the basic idea is the same. A generator uses magnets and wires to turn mechanical energy into electrical energy.

How Generators Are Powered

Generators can make electrical energy in many ways. Generators can use the energy of wind, or, in some cases, it can use the energy of falling water. Other generators are powered by steam or by nuclear energy heating the water. In each generator, mechanical energy spins wires around a magnet.

Electrical Safety

Electricity lights homes, cooks food, and powers machines. But you must be careful when using electricity. It can cause a shock or start a fire.

To be safe, you should read and follow instructions that come with every electrical product you use. Replace electrical cords that are old or cracked. Be sure to move cords so that people will not walk on or trip over them.

Lesson 5 Checkpoint

1. What happens when a magnet is moved back and forth inside a coiled wire?

_____

_____

2. How do magnets help generators create electricity?

_____

_____

Use with pp. 407-411

Lesson 1: What is sound energy?

Vocabulary

compression the part of a wave where the particles are bunched together

frequency the number of waves that pass a point in a certain amount of time

wavelength the distance between a point on one wave and a similar point on the next wave

Sound is a form of energy that travels in waves. Sound occurs when objects vibrate. A vibration is a quick back-and-forth movement. For example, a guitar string will vibrate if you pluck it. The string passes energy to the air around it. These vibrations move through the air as sound waves. We hear the guitar's sound when the sound waves reach our ears.

Types of Sound Waves

A sound wave causes air particles to move. These particles form a pattern. Groups of particles bunch together. This part of the wave is called a **compression**. There are groups of particles that are far apart.

Scientists classify waves based on the how they travel. There are two major kinds of waves, transverse waves and longitudinal waves.

In a transverse wave, the particles in the material and the wave travel in different directions. Think about a jump rope. The wave travels toward the jumper, but the rope moves up and down.

In a longitudinal wave, the particles in the material and the wave travel in the same direction. The particles in the material vibrate from left to right when the wave moves from left to right. Sound waves are longitudinal waves.

Waves can travel in different ways. But, all waves have certain properties. Frequency and wavelength are two of these properties. The **frequency** of a wave is the number of vibrations a wave makes in a certain amount of time. A wave's frequency is higher when the wave vibrates faster. **Wavelength** is the distance between a point on one wave and a similar point on the next wave.

How Sound Travels

Sound waves need a medium in which to travel. Gases, liquids, and solids are mediums. Sound waves travel at different speeds through different mediums. How fast sound moves through a medium depends on how tightly the medium's particles are packed.

A solid's particles are close together. This means a sound wave's vibrations can quickly move from one particle to the next.

Particles are farther apart in a liquid. Vibrations take a little longer to move from one particle to another. So, sound waves travel slower in a liquid than in a solid.

Particles are farthest apart in a gas. The vibrations take longer to move from particle to particle. A sound wave moves slowest in a gas.

Sound waves can bump into things when they travel. If you shout your name into a cave, the sound waves will bounce off the cave wall. They travel back to you. You will hear your name repeated. This reflected sound is called an echo.

Quick Study

Lesson 1 Checkpoint

1. What is sound?

_____

_____

2. What are two types of wave?

_____

_____

3. Why does sound travel fastest in solids and slowest in gases?

_____

_____

_____

4. How does an echo form?

_____

_____

5. **Draw Conclusions** A bird perched in a tree hears the chirping of another bird. A whale hears the song-like sound made by another whale swimming near it. Which sound travels faster, the bird's chirping or the whale's singing? Explain how you decided.

_____

_____

_____

Lesson 2: How is sound made?

Vocabulary

pitch what makes a sound seem high or low

Loudness

Loudness is a measure of how strong a sound seems to be. Loudness is related to the amount of energy in a sound wave. You may whisper softly to a friend in the library. But you may shout at a baseball game. The shout is much louder than the whisper.

Sound waves spread out as they move. This means that a sound will not seem as loud if you are far from the source of a sound. For instance, a dog barking across the street sounds softer than a dog barking right next to you.

Pitch

Pitch is what makes a sound seem high or low. Pitch depends on a sound's frequency. Objects that vibrate quickly have high frequencies. Objects with high frequencies have a high pitch. Objects that vibrate slowly have a low frequency and a low pitch. The material of the object making the sound affects the sound you hear. The size and shape of the object also affects the sound.

How Instruments Make Sound

Guitars, violins, and harps are examples of string instruments. String instruments make sound when a musician plucks, rubs, or hits the strings. This sends vibrations through the instrument.

Strings on a guitar are stretched between the top and bottom of the instrument. A guitarist plays notes by plucking the strings. The note a guitarist plays depends on how tightly the string is stretched. Tighter strings make sounds with higher pitches. Looser strings make sounds with lower pitches.

The note a guitarist plays also depends on the length and thickness of the string. Sound waves travel slowest through the thicker, heavier strings. These strings vibrate slowest and play the lowest pitches. Waves travel more quickly through the thinner strings. They vibrate faster and have higher pitches.

Percussion Instruments

Drums, xylophones, and maracas are examples of percussion instruments. Percussion instruments make sounds when something like a hand or a stick hits them. For example, a drum vibrates and makes a sound when you hit it.

Wind Instruments

Recorders and flutes are examples of wind instruments. Wind instruments make sounds when a musician blows air across a hole. This makes the particles in a column of air vibrate. Shorter instruments have a shorter column of air. This means that shorter instruments make sounds with higher pitches.

The Piano

A piano has over 200 strings. Each key on a piano matches a group of strings. Pressing a key makes a padded hammer strike the group of strings. The strings vibrate. This makes a sound. Pressing the piano keys harder will not change the sound's frequency or pitch. Pressing the piano keys harder will make the sound louder.

Lesson 2 Checkpoint

1. What type of pitch does a high-frequency sound have?

   _____

2. How does a wind instrument produce sound?

   _____

   _____

3. How does the pitch of a thick guitar string compare to that of a thinner string?

   _____

   _____

4. **Draw Conclusions** By shortening or tightening a guitar string, you raise the pitch. What do you conclude will happen to the pitch if you tighten the skin stretched across the top of a drum?

   _____

   _____

Lesson 3: What is light energy?

Sources of Light

Light is a form of energy. The Sun, a bonfire, and a street lamp are some sources of light energy. The Sun is the most important light source to Earth. Earth would be a dead planet without the Sun. Earth would be too cold and dark for humans, plants, and animals to survive.

Some animals give off light. This is called bioluminescence. The light comes from inside the animal's body. Some sea animals that live near the bottom of the ocean are bioluminescent.

Humans discovered long ago that they can also make light. Using fire allows humans to cook, stay warm, and work after dark.

Shadows

Light travels in straight lines called rays that fan out from the source of the light. You can easily see how light travels by looking at a shadow. Hold your hand in front of a wall. Shine a flashlight on it. Your hand will block the light rays. A dark area will appear. This is a shadow. The size of the shadow can change. The shadow will get bigger if you move your hand closer to the flashlight, The shadow will get smaller if you move your hand away from the flashlight.

The angle that light hits an object also affects the size of the shadow. Think of your own shadow on a sunny day. The Sun is high in the sky at noon. This is when your shadow is short. Your shadow is longer when the Sun is lower in the sky.

Light Waves We See

The light we see is called visible light. Visible light makes up only a tiny part of all light energy. Scientists call all forms of light energy electromagnetic radiation.

Light energy travels as a wave. Light waves have wavelengths and frequencies. These wavelengths and frequencies control the colors of the light we see. Humans can only see the colors in the visible spectrum: red, orange, yellow, green, blue, and violet. Red light is always on the left side of the spectrum because red light has the longest wavelength and the lowest frequency. Violet light is always on the right side of the spectrum because it has the shortest wavelength and the highest frequency. Light waves with the same wavelengths all have the same color.

Light Waves We Cannot See

Most waves in the electromagnetic spectrum cannot be seen. Radio waves and microwaves cannot be seen. Their wavelengths are too long for the human eye to see. X-rays cannot be seen because their wavelengths are too short.

Scientists use special tools to study waves that we cannot see. These waves act like waves we can see. All electromagnetic waves act the same way. They all travel at the same speed through empty space. They all carry energy that can be absorbed by an object and then changed to another form of energy, such as heat.

Large amounts of high-energy waves can hurt cells. Ultraviolet waves from the Sun can harm your eyes. High-energy waves can be helpful. For example, small amounts of ultraviolet waves can kill bacteria. Microwaves can cook food. X-rays can show a doctor a patient's broken bone.

© Pearson Education, Inc. 4

Quick Study

Name _____

Lesson 3 Checkpoint

1. What do the Sun, a bonfire, and a street lamp have in common?

_____

2. What colors of light make up the visible spectrum?

_____

_____

3. Why can't humans see X-rays?

_____

_____

4. **Draw Conclusions** Laser light waves all have the same wavelength. What can you conclude about the color of laser light?

_____

_____

Lesson 4: How do light and matter interact?

Vocabulary

reflection when light rays bounce, or reflect, from the surface back to our eyes

absorption when an object takes in a light wave

transparent materials that transmit nearly all of the light rays that hit them

translucent materials that let some light rays pass through but scatter other rays

opaque materials that do not let any light pass through them

refraction bending of light caused by a change of speed

Light waves reflect a little off most objects. **Reflection** occurs when light rays bounce off a surface. Some objects reflect almost all light rays that hit them, like a mirror. Light waves can also be absorbed. **Absorption** occurs when an object takes in the light wave. Then, the wave becomes heat energy.

You can see colors because objects absorb some frequencies of light and reflect others. A blue shirt looks blue because if reflects blue frequency light waves. It absorbs other visible light rays. An object looks black when it absorbs all the colors of the visible spectrum. An object looks white when all the colors of the visible spectrum are reflected.

Materials that let the light rays pass through them are **transparent.** You can clearly what is on the other side of transparent material. Clean water and windows are transparent.

Materials that let some light pass through but scatter other rays are **translucent.** Objects on the other side of a translucent material look blurry. Waxed paper is a translucent material.

Materials that do not let any light pass through are **opaque.** You cannot see through an opaque object. An opaque material either reflects or absorbs light rays. Aluminum foil is an opaque material that reflects light. Wood is an opaque material that absorbs light.

Light does not need to a medium to travel through. Light travels fastest through the empty space of a vacuum, like in outer space. Light slows a little when it travels through different mediums. Suppose light waves travel from a vacuum to a gas. The light wave slows down as it hits the gas.

Particles in a liquid are closer together than particles in a gas. So, light travels through a liquid slower than through a gas. Particles in a solid are closer together than particles in a liquid. Light moves slowest through solids.

Light changes speed as it moves from one transparent medium to another. This change in speed causes light to bend. This bending is **refraction.**

Lenses are curved pieces of clear glass or plastic that bend light that pass through them. There are two main kinds of lenses, convex and concave.

A convex lens is thicker in the middle than at the edges. Light rays bend toward the middle when light passes through. A convex lens makes things look bigger. Microscopes have convex lenses.

A concave lens is thinner in the middle. Light rays bend toward the thicker edges when light passes through. A concave lens makes things look smaller.

© Pearson Education, Inc. 4

Quick Study

Lesson 4 Checkpoint

1. How does light behave when it strikes a transparent object?

_____

2. In which medium does light travel faster, a gas or a liquid?

_____

3. What happens to light energy when it is absorbed by an object?

_____

_____

4. What does a convex lens look like?

_____

5. **Draw Conclusions** What happens when light rays strike a mirror?

_____

_____

Lesson 1: What is motion?

Vocabulary

relative motion change in one object's position compared to position of another fixed object

frame of reference the objects you use to detect motion

speed the rate at which an object changes position

velocity the speed and the direction of an object

Types of Motion

Objects can move in different ways. One way objects can move is in a straight line. A baseball player running to home plate usually moves in a straight line.

Objects can also move in a curved path. The wheels on your bicycle follow a curved path around the center of the wheel.

Objects can also move back and forth. When a guitar player plucks a string, the string moves back and forth.

When you ride your bicycle, you pass many things that do not move. They are fixed in place. When you ride your bicycle past a mailbox you know you are moving. You compare things that change position with things that do not change position. The change in one object's position compared to another object's fixed position is **relative motion.**

How You Know You Are Moving

How do you know if a person on a slide moves? You look at the changing position of the person. You compare the changing position with the fixed position of the slide. You use the relative motion of the objects to decide what is moving and what is not moving.

The objects you use to decide if something is moving are your **frame of reference.** Your frame of reference is like your point of view.

Imagine you are on a moving school bus. From your frame of reference on the bus, the buildings outside seem to be moving. But the buildings have not moved. As the bus moves down the street, people on the sidewalk see you on the bus. From their frame of reference, you and the bus are both moving.

Measuring Motion

Speed is the rate at which an object changes position. It measures how fast an object moves. A car moving at a high speed changes position faster than a car moving at a slower speed. The unit for speed is a unit of distance divided by a unit of time. Kilometers per hour is a unit of speed.

Velocity is the speed and direction an object is moving. Direction can be described using different words. *North, south, east,* and *west* can describe direction. *Up, down, right,* and *left* can also describe direction.

Any change in the speed or direction of an object's motion is acceleration. Speeding up and slowing down are accelerations. A roller coaster accelerates as it moves up a hill because it is changing speed. A roller coaster accelerates on a curved path because it changes direction.

Quick Study

Lesson 1 Checkpoint

1. What are three different types of motion?

_____

_____

_____

2. **Sequence** Describe the sequence of events of the yellow race car as it travels around the track on page 439.

_____

_____

3. What is a frame of reference?

_____

_____

4. What are two ways that a roller coaster can accelerate?

_____

_____

Lesson 2: How does force affect moving objects?

Vocabulary

force any push or pull

friction a force that acts when two surfaces rub together

Force

A **force** is any push or pull. Force can make an object start or stop moving. Force can make a moving object speed up, slow down, or change direction.

A contact force must touch an object to affect its movement. A marble on a table will not roll until it is hit. Other forces can affect objects without touching them. For example, a magnet can pull a piece of iron towards it without touching it.

A force can change the position and the motion of an object. The size of the change depends on the strength of the force. The harder you kick a ball, the faster and farther it will go.

Combining Forces

All forces have both size and direction. During a tug-of-war, the teams are combining forces, but, they are working against each other. They are pulling in opposite directions. As long as both teams pull with the same force, the forces are balanced. The tug-of-war rope will not move. But if one team pulls with more force, the forces will become unbalanced. The team that pulls with the greater force will win.

Many objects are acted upon by more than one force. If you push a door while your friend pushes it, the door moves quickly. This is because both forces were acting on the door in the same direction. The total force on the door can be found by adding the forces together.

Force and Motion

An object will not start moving unless the forces acting on it change. The resistance an object has to any change to its motion is called inertia.

A moving object will not change direction or speed unless the forces acting on it change.

The amount of force acting on an object affects how the object changes speed and direction. Think about riding your bicycle. If you peddle faster, the bicycle moves faster.

More force is needed to move heavier objects than lighter objects. It is easier to pull an empty wagon than a wagon with a person sitting in it.

Friction

Friction is a force that acts when two surfaces rub together. Friction can slow or stop moving objects. A greater amount of friction means you need more force to move an object.

When objects with rough surfaces rub, they catch on each other. This causes a lot of friction. When objects with smooth surfaces rub, the objects move easily. There is less friction.

The amount of friction also depends on the mass of each object. A box of books is harder to move than a box of feathers. The box of books presses against the floor with more force. This causes more friction, and the box is harder to push.

© Pearson Education, Inc. 4

Lesson 2 Checkpoint

1. What causes objects to move or moving objects to stop moving?

_____

2. ⊙ **Sequence** Describe the sequence of events if the dog on the right on page 443 suddenly stops pulling on the toy.

_____

_____

_____

3. What is friction?

_____

_____

Name _____

Lesson 3: How are force, mass, and energy related?

Vocabulary

gravity the force that makes objects pull toward each other

work the ability to move something

kinetic energy the energy of motion

potential energy stored energy

The Force of Gravity

When a pencil rolls off a desk, it falls to the ground. A force acts on the pencil to make it fall. That force is **gravity.** Gravity makes objects pull towards each other.

The force of gravity is stronger when objects are close together. As the objects move farther apart, the force of gravity becomes weaker. The force of gravity between massive objects is strong. The force of gravity becomes weaker when the mass of the objects is less.

Measuring Force

A spring scale is a tool used to measure force. It has a hook on the bottom. When you hang an object from the hook, the spring stretches. How far the spring stretches depends on an object's weight. The more an object weighs, the stronger the force and the more the spring will stretch. As the spring stretches, a marker moves along numbers on the scale. These numbers are the unit of force called the newton. One newton (1 N) is about the amount of force needed to lift a small apple.

Energy and Motion

Work is the ability to move something. When work is done, a change happens. Energy makes the change happen.

The energy of motion is **kinetic energy.** All moving things have kinetic energy. The amount of kinetic energy is based on an object's speed and mass. An empty wagon moving at 2 miles per hour has less kinetic energy than a full wagon moving at 3 miles per hour.

Stored Energy

Potential energy is stored energy. When you hold a yo-yo in your hand it has potential energy. As soon as you let go of the yo-yo, it starts using its potential energy. Objects that are stretched or squeezed also have potential energy. A stretched rubber band has potential energy. The tightened spring on a wind-up toy also has potential energy.

Changing Types of Energy

Potential energy can change to kinetic energy. Kinetic energy can change back to potential energy. Think of a wind-up toy bird. Each turn winds the spring tighter. This adds more potential energy. When you release the toy, the spring unwinds. The bird moves forward. The potential energy in the spring is changing into kinetic energy.

Think about the swings on the playground. At the top of the swing's path, the swing has potential energy. As it moves towards the ground, the stored energy changes into the energy of motion. Then, as the swing moves back toward the sky, the energy of motion changes into stored energy. The process continues until you get off the swing.

© Pearson Education, Inc. 4

Name _____

Lesson 3 Checkpoint

1. What two factors affect the force of gravity between two objects?

   _____

   _____

2. What kind of energy does a stretched rubber band have?

   _____

3. How is energy changed in the toy bird?

   _____

   _____

Lesson 1: What is a machine?

Vocabulary

lever a simple machine made of a long bar with a support

fulcrum the support part of a lever

load the weight that is to be lifted or moved

effort the force, or push or pull, used on the bar

wheel and axle a simple machine made of a wheel and a rod

pulley a wheel with a rope, wire, or chain around it

Machines and Work

Some machines only have one part. Other machines have many parts. All machines help us do work. Work means using force to move an object or make a change.

Machines make work easier. Some simple machines allow you to use less force to do work, or change the direction of the force you use. You can push or pull in one direction and get work done in a different direction. The lever, the pulley, the inclined plane, the wheel and axle, the wedge, and the screw are all simple machines.

Levers

A lever is a long bar with a support. The support is called a **fulcrum.** A fulcrum holds the weight of the bar and what the bar carries. The object you want to lift or move is the **load.** You have to use some effort in order to use a lever. The **effort** is a push or pull on the bar that makes the load move in some way. A lever makes work easier by adding to your force.

Different kinds of levers do different jobs. You can use a lever with a fulcrum that is halfway between the load and the effort to change the direction of the force. You can also use a lever with a fulcrum that is closer to the load than to the effort. This lever lets you lift a heavier object.

Wheel and Axle

A **wheel and axle** moves or turns objects. The axle is a rod that goes through the center of the wheel. A screwdriver is a wheel and axle. The handle is the wheel. The blade is the axle. The end of the blade fits into a slot on the screw. The force you use to turn the handle increases. The blade turns and tightens the screw.

Pulley

A **pulley** is a wheel with a rope, wire, or chain around it. A fixed pulley stays in one place. It uses gravity to help lift a load. The bottom is a moveable pulley. It moves up or down with the load. The load hangs from a hook.

We use pulleys to change the direction of the force. Pretend you want to raise something. You would have to pull down on the pulley. This is changing the direction of force.

We can use pulleys to lessen the amount of force needed to lift a load. This is true only when two or more pulleys are used together. A second rope, wire, or chain is used between the pulleys. This rope, wire, or chain can carry more weight. The person or machine working the pulley uses less force to lift the load. We can use many pulleys at the same time to lift a very heavy load. You use much less effort than you would without the pulleys.

Lesson 1 Checkpoint

1. How do you use force to do work?

   _____

   _____

2. Define fulcrum, load, and effort.

   _____

   _____

   _____

3. How does an axle fit into a wheel?

   _____

   _____

4. How does a fixed pulley help you lift a load?

   _____

   _____

5. **Summarize** How many ways can you use pulleys? Briefly describe at least three ways.

   _____

   _____

   _____

Lesson 2: How can machines work together?

Vocabulary

inclined plane a simple machine such as a ramp

wedge a simple machine made of two inclined planes put together

screw a small stick with slanting ridges called threads wrapped around it

Inclined Plane

A ramp is a simple machine called an inclined plane. You use more force to lift an object straight up than when you slide it up to the same level on an **inclined plane.** An inclined plane allows people to use less force over a greater distance.

Factors That Affect Force

Inclined planes help move objects up or down. Different factors affect how much force is needed to move an object. One factor is how steep the inclined plane is. If there are two ramps that are the same height, a greater force is needed to move an object up the steeper ramp.

Friction also affects how much force is needed to move an object. Friction is a force between two objects that touch and rub. Friction makes it harder to push, drag, or slide things. A box with wheels will take away most of the friction.

A third factor that affects force is the weight of the object. More force is needed to move a heavier object.

Wedges

A **wedge** is one kind of inclined plane. A wedge is like two inclined planes put together. A force used on one end of the wedge pushes the inclined planes into an object. Wedges can be used to split things apart or move things. Axes are used to split logs. Wedges can also be used to hold things in place, like a nail.

Screws

A **screw** is another simple machine. A screw has ridges around it. These ridges are called threads. You would see an inclined plane if you unwrapped these threads. A screw is a kind of inclined plane.

Screws hold things together such as pieces of wood. Screws can also be used to lift things. You could pull on the screw to lift the wood. The screw's threads make it hard to pull it out. A special screw called an auger is used to drill holes.

Complex Machines

Complex machines are machines that have many parts. A can opener is a complex machine. Many complex machines are made of simple machines that work together. What kind of simple machine is the edge of a can opener? It is a wedge. What kind of simple machine do you think the long handles are? The long handles are levers. The winding handle is part of a wheel and axle.

A lawnmower is another complex machine. Its tires are an example of a wheel and axle. Its blade is a kind of wedge.

Some complex machines have different sources of power. Your muscles work to use the can opener and the lawnmower. Some complex machines use solar energy. They change energy from the Sun into electricity.

© Pearson Education, Inc. 4

Quick Study

Lesson 2 Checkpoint

1. You move a heavy box up an inclined plane, farther than if you lifted it straight up to the same height. Is using the inclined plane a good idea? Explain your answer.

   _____

   _____

   _____

2. What part does an inclined plane play in a wedge? in a screw?

   _____

   _____

3. Name three kinds of work that a screw can do. Give an example of each.

   _____

   _____

   _____

4. What is a complex machine?

   _____

5. **Summarize** Write two or three questions that would help you summarize what you know about a can opener.

   _____

   _____

   _____

Lesson 1: How does Earth move?

Vocabulary

axis an imaginary line that goes through an object's center

rotation the spinning of a planet, moon, or star around its axis

revolution the repeated motion of one object around another, much more massive object

orbit path followed by one object as it revolves around another object

ellipse oval-shaped curve like a circle stretched out in two opposite directions

Earth Seems to Stand Still

Earth is always moving. We do not feel it because we are moving along with Earth. Also, Earth moves very smoothly. There are some clues that Earth is moving. The first clue is that the Sun and stars seem to move across the sky. This happens because the Earth is turning. The second clue is that the seasons change during the year. These changes are partly caused by the way Earth moves in space. Scientists use many tools to study how the stars and other objects seem to move.

Earth's Rotation

Earth turns around an imaginary pole through its center called its **axis.** Earth spinning around its axis is called rotation. Earth takes about a day to make one **rotation.** Earth rotates from west to east. This makes objects like the Sun and stars seem to move from east to west in the sky.

Why Shadows Change

Shadows form when light shines on an object but does not pass through it. Earth's rotation causes sunlight to shine on objects from different angles throughout the day. This causes the length and position of an object's shadow to change. Earth's rotation causes day and night. When Earth is turned towards the Sun, it is daytime. It is nighttime when Earth is turned away from the Sun.

Daylight Hours

The number of daylight hours changes during the year. The Northern Hemisphere has more daylight hours during the summer months and fewer daylight hours during the winter months.

Earth's Revolution

The movement of one object around another is called a **revolution.** It takes Earth about one year to revolve around the Sun. The path Earth takes around the Sun is its **orbit.** Gravity is a force that pulls two objects towards each other. Gravity between the Earth and the Sun keeps the Earth in its orbit. Earth's orbit is an **ellipse.** An ellipse looks like a circle that is stretched out.

Earth's Tilted Axis

Earth's axis always tilts in the same direction. The tilt affects how places on Earth receive sunlight. This is what causes Earth's seasons. The Northern Hemisphere gets more direct sunlight when it tilts towards the Sun in the summer. Daylight lasts longer. Temperatures are higher. At the same time, it is winter in the Southern Hemisphere as it tilts away from the Sun. The days are shorter. The temperatures are lower.

© Pearson Education, Inc. 4

Name _____

Lesson 1 Checkpoint

1. Why does the Earth seem to be standing still?

_____

_____

2. Why do the Sun and the stars appear to move from east to west in the sky?

_____

_____

3. Why is it summer in the Northern Hemisphere when it is winter in the Southern Hemisphere?

_____

_____

4. **Cause and Effect** Explain what causes Earth's seasons.

_____

_____

Lesson 2: What patterns can you see in the sky?

Vocabulary

eclipse when one object in space casts its shadow on another

lunar eclipse the passage of the Moon through Earth's shadow

solar eclipse when the Moon casts its shadow on Earth

constellations the 88 star patterns in the sky used to identify and name the stars

Sun, Moon, and Earth

The Moon does not make its own light. You can see the Moon because sunlight reflects off the Moon's surface. The Moon orbits around Earth. Its orbit is shaped like an ellipse. It takes about 29 days to revolve around Earth. The Moon rotates once around its axis as it revolves around the Earth. This is why the same side of the Moon always faces Earth.

The Moon's shape seems to change at different times of the month. All the Moon's shapes are called the phases of the Moon. These phases are caused by the Moon's revolution around Earth. Half of the Moon faces the Sun. We only see the part of the Moon that reflects the Sun. The Moon looks like a circle when its lighted half faces Earth. This is called a Full Moon. Then, only parts of the lighted half of the Moon face Earth and the Moon appears to have different shapes. Then you cannot see the Moon at all. The pattern begins again.

Eclipses

An **eclipse** occurs when one object in space gets between the Sun and another object. This causes a shadow to fall on the second object.

A **lunar eclipse** is when the Moon passes through Earth's shadow. A partial eclipse is when only part of the Moon is in Earth's shadow. Then, the Moon might look like something took a bite out of it. Unlike a partial eclipse, a total lunar eclipse occurs when the whole Moon is in the Earth's shadow. The Moon does not disappear during a lunar eclipse. Earth's atmosphere bends and scatters some sunlight, allowing some of the Sun's rays to reach the Moon. Lunar eclipses happen several times a year.

A **solar eclipse** is when the Moon moves between the Sun and Earth. This causes the Moon's shadow to fall on Earth. It can only be seen where the moon casts its shadow.

Stars

There are many, many stars in the sky. The Sun is the star nearest to Earth. The Sun gives energy and light and is a hot ball of gas. Some stars are bigger, brighter, or hotter than the Sun, and some are smaller, dimmer, and cooler. We cannot see other stars during the day because the Sun is so bright.

The patterns of stars in the sky are called **constellations.** Some stars in each constellation are closer to Earth than others. We cannot see the distance between these stars. This is why the stars in each constellation look like they are close together. They appear to move in the sky as Earth rotates. People who live in the Southern Hemisphere see different constellations than people in the Northern Hemisphere.

© Pearson Education, Inc. 4

Lesson 2 Checkpoint

1. What causes the apparent repeated changes of the Moon's shape?

_____

_____

2. How is a total lunar eclipse different from other lunar eclipses?

_____

_____

3. Why does the Moon remain partly visible during a lunar eclipse?

_____

_____

4. Why do distant stars that are actually very far from each other appear to be close together in the sky?

_____

_____

5. 🎯 **Cause and Effect** What kinds of motion cause solar and lunar eclipses? Explain.

_____

_____

Name _____

Lesson 1: What makes up the universe?

Vocabulary

universe all of space and the objects that exist in space

galaxy a system of billions of stars, gases, and dust clustered together

astronomy the study of the Sun, Moon, stars, and other objects in space

solar system planets, their moons, and other objects that revolve
around the Sun

The Universe and the Milky Way

The **universe** is all of space and everything in it. Most of the universe is empty space. The universe has millions of galaxies. A **galaxy** is a system of stars, gases, and dust clustered together. We live in the Milky Way galaxy. Our Sun is one of billions of stars in our galaxy.

People have always watched objects move across the sky. The study of the Sun, Moon, stars, and other objects in space is **astronomy.** The Greeks, Arabs, Indians, and other early civilizations used astronomy to decide when to plant and harvest crops. Sailors used the Sun and stars to tell them where they were.

Our Solar System

The **solar system** includes the Sun, the planets, their moons, and other objects. Everything in the solar system revolves around the Sun. A planet is a very large, ball-shaped object that revolves around a star, such as the Sun. Planets are cooler and smaller than stars. Planets do not give off their own light. They reflect the light from the star they orbit.

Our solar system has nine planets that are divided into two groups. The inner planets are Mercury, Venus, Earth, and Mars. The outer planets are Jupiter, Saturn, Uranus, Neptune, and Pluto. An area called the asteroid belt is between the inner planets and outer planets. An asteroid is a small rocky object that orbits the Sun. Asteroids are too small to be called planets. The asteroid belt is made of many asteroids.

Gravity is the force that keeps the Earth and other objects in their orbits. Planets usually move in straight lines. But the pull of the Sun's gravity is strong. It pulls the planets towards the Sun. This causes the planets to move in curved paths around the Sun. The orbits of planets are elliptical, or shaped like slightly flattened circles.

The Sun

Our Sun is a medium sized star but it is the largest body in the solar system. It is a huge ball of hot, glowing gases. The Sun's energy heats and lights Earth.

Like Earth, the Sun has magnetism. The Sun's magnetic field can be very strong in some places. Large loops of gas can reach out from the Sun's surface in these areas. Dark spots called sunspots appear at places where the magnetic field is strong.

Lesson 1 Checkpoint

1. Describe what makes up the universe.

_____

_____

2. Why do planets orbit around the Sun?

_____

_____

3. Name three different types of objects in our solar system.

_____

_____

_____

Lesson 2: What are the inner planets?

Vocabulary

craters large dents shaped like bowls on the surface of a planet

space probe a vehicle that carries cameras and other tools for studying objects in space

satellite an object that orbits another object in space

Mercury

Mercury is the planet closest to the Sun. It is a little bigger than Earth's moon. Mercury has dents all over it called **craters.** Craters were made when rocks from space crashed into Mercury's surface long ago. Mercury has almost no atmosphere. Its daytime temperatures are four to five times hotter than the hottest place on Earth. This is because Mercury is so close to the Sun. Mercury gets very cold at night because there is no atmosphere to hold in the heat.

Venus

Venus is the second planet from the Sun. It is about the same size as Earth. Like Mercury, people could not live on Venus. This planet is also very hot and dry. Unlike Mercury, Venus has an atmosphere. It is made of clouds that are burning hot and poisonous. These clouds reflect the Sun's light. Venus is one of the brightest objects in the night sky.

Earth

Earth is the third planet from the Sun. It is the only planet with liquid water on its surface. Earth is wrapped in a layer of gas. This is Earth's atmosphere. The atmosphere makes life possible on Earth. It protects us from some of the Sun's harmful rays. The atmosphere has nitrogen, oxygen, carbon dioxide, and water vapor in it. Plants and animals use these gases to live. Earth is the only planet in the solar system that has living things on it.

The Moon

A moon is a **satellite**. A satellite is an object that orbits another object in space. The gravity between a planet and its moon keeps the moon in orbit. Earth has one large Moon. It is about one-fourth the size of Earth and has no atmosphere. Its surface is covered with many craters. The Soviet Union sent the first **space probes** to the Moon in 1959. In 1961, the Soviet Union sent the first person into space. In 1969, Americans Neil Armstrong and Buzz Aldrin were the first people to walk on the Moon.

Mars

Mars, fourth planet from the Sun, has rocks and soil that contain the mineral iron oxide. It has a reddish-brown color. This is why the planet's nickname is the "Red Planet." Mars has two moons. The atmosphere on Mars cannot support living beings. Winds on Mars cause dust storms that sometimes cover the whole planet. Like Earth, Mars has polar caps, volcanoes and a canyon. Its canyon is bigger than the Grand Canyon on Earth. Scientists want to learn about the materials that make up Mars. They are using Rovers to find out if Mars has or once had water. If so, scientists may predict that living beings once lived on Mars.

© Pearson Education, Inc. 4

Lesson 2 Checkpoint

1. What are some reasons why people cannot live on Mercury or Venus?

_____

_____

_____

2. What makes life possible on Earth?

_____

_____

3. Why is the soil on Mars red?

_____

_____

4. What characteristics do Earth and Mars have in common?

_____

_____

5. **Predict** What might scientists predict if the Rovers find water on Mars?

_____

_____

_____

© Pearson Education, Inc. 4

Lesson 3: What do we know about Jupiter, Saturn, and Uranus?

Jupiter

Jupiter is the fifth planet from the Sun. Jupiter is a gas giant. A gas giant is a very large planet made mostly of gases. Jupiter is the largest planet in our solar system.

Jupiter's atmosphere is mainly made of hydrogen and helium. This atmosphere has a weather system called the Great Red Spot.

Jupiter's Moons

Jupiter has many moons. Io is the name of one moon. Io has more active volcanoes than any other object in the solar system. Europa is another moon. Europa is the smoothest object in the solar system and has a frozen crust. An ocean might be under this crust. Scientists think there may be living organisms on Europa. Ganymede is the largest moon in the solar system. Callisto is also a moon. It has more craters than any other object in the solar system.

Saturn

Saturn is the sixth planet from the Sun. Saturn is a gas giant, like Jupiter, and its atmosphere is also mostly hydrogen and helium.

Saturn is best known for its brilliant rings. The rings around Saturn are made of water, ice, dust, and chunks of rock. These particles range in size from tiny grains of sand to boulders.

Galileo's Handles

Galileo was an astronomer. He invented an astronomical telescope to look at the Moon and planets. Galileo was surprised when he saw Saturn. He saw what looked like a planet with handles! The "handles" were actually the rings that orbit Saturn.

Moons of Saturn

Saturn has a least 31 moons. Most of its moons are small. Titan is one of Saturn's moons. Titan has an atmosphere. It is also larger than both Mercury and Pluto.

Uranus

Uranus is the seventh planet from the Sun. This gas giant is the farthest planet you can see without a telescope. Uranus has an atmosphere like other gas giants made of hydrogen and helium. Unlike Jupiter and Saturn, however, this atmosphere is also made of methane. Uranus is so cold that the methane is a liquid. This liquid methane forms a thin cloud that covers the planet. This makes Uranus look blue-green. Like other gas giants, Uranus has a ring system and many moons.

Rolling Through Space

Uranus rotates on its side. Scientists think that a large object may have hit Uranus when the solar system was forming. This bump may have tilted Uranus onto its side.

The Moons of Uranus

Uranus has at least 27 moons. Some of the moons are hard to see without strong telescopes. The moons closer to the planet are larger moons with deep valleys, craters, and steep ridges.

Lesson 3 Checkpoint

1. What is a gas giant?

_____

2. What are Saturn's rings made of?

_____

3. How is the atmosphere of Uranus different from that of Saturn?

_____

_____

4. How is Uranus different from other gas giants?

_____

_____

_____

Lesson 4: What do we know about Neptune, Pluto, and beyond?

Neptune

Neptune is the eighth planet from the Sun. It is the smallest of the gas giants. But it is still so big it could hold about 60 Earths. We cannot see Neptune without a telescope because it is so far away.

Neptune's orbit around the Sun takes more than one hundred years. This is because Neptune is so far from the Sun. Neptune is a windy planet. It has a storm called The Great Dark Spot. Neptune's winds blow the Great Dark Spot across the planet.

How Neptune Was Discovered

British Astronomer John Couch Adams observed that Uranus was not orbiting the way he thought it should. Adams thought that the gravity from another planet was affecting Uranus' orbit. Mathematician Urbain Leverrier was another researcher. He used math to predict the position and size of this other planet. He shared his findings with other astronomers. In 1846, astronomer Johann Galle used Leverrier's information to find Neptune.

The Moons of Neptune

Neptune has at least 13 moons. The largest moon is Triton. It may be the coldest object in the solar system. Astronomers think Triton didn't form with Neptune but formed farther from the Sun. They think Triton was captured by Neptune's gravity.

Pluto

The size of the planets varies greatly. The largest planet is Jupiter. It is followed by Saturn, Uranus, Neptune, Earth, Venus, Mars, and Mercury. Pluto is the smallest planet in the solar system. It is even smaller than Earth's moon. It is the ninth planet from the Sun. Pluto is the only outer planet that is not a gas giant. It has an icy, solid surface.

Pluto has one moon called Charon. Many astronomers think of Pluto and Charon as a double planet system because they are so close together and very close in size.

An Odd Orbit

Pluto has an odd orbit. The other planets travel around the Sun at the same angle. Pluto's orbit is tilted. During part of its orbit, Pluto is closer to the Sun than Neptune.

Sedna

Is Sedna the tenth planet? Sedna was discovered in 2003. It is smaller than Earth's moon. Living beings could not live on Sedna. It is as far as 84 billion miles from the Sun. Sedna's daytime summer temperature is a chilly -240°C.

Quick Study

Name _____

Lesson 4 Review

Use with pp. 534-537

Lesson 4 Checkpoint

1. How does Neptune compare in size with other planets?

_____

_____

2. List the planets in order from the smallest to the largest.

_____

_____

3. 🎯 **Predict** Will astronomers find evidence of life on Sedna?

_____

© Pearson Education, Inc. 4

Quick Study

Chapter 18, Lesson 4 Review **121**

Name _____

Lesson 1: How does technology affect our lives?

Vocabulary

technology the knowledge, processes, and products we use to solve problems and make work easier

optical fibers very thin tubes that allow light to pass through them

Creating New Challenges

Technology is the knowledge, processes, and products that we use to solve problems and make our work easier.

Technology has had a huge effect on living things. Some products of technology hurt people, animals, and plants. Examples are car fumes, industrial waste, and insect poisons. The United States and other countries have air, water, and soil pollution because of these side effects.

New technologies can change the way people do their jobs. Some technology can do things people once did. This means that people can lose their jobs. But technologies can also create jobs.

Technology and Materials

In-line skating gear is made from many different materials. The skates are made from rubber, plastic, metal, and nylon. Some of these are natural resources and others have been created using technology.

Technology also helps keep us safe and healthy. An inline skater wears a helmet, knee pads, elbow pads, and wrist guards. Technology was used to design and make this equipment.

From Hitchhiker to Invention

A burr is an item found in nature. It is prickly with tiny hooks. Burrs easily attach to things. One day, an engineer got the idea to make sticky fastener called Velcro™. It is used in clothing, medical equipment, and sports gear.

Controlling Waste

Many companies are working to make products out of things that will decompose and become part of Earth again.

Materials that are not a part of nature may not break down as easily. People have used technology to make them. Plastic, glass, aluminum, and other materials made through technology should be recycled.

Technology and Medicine

Medical technology has changed the tools doctors use during surgery. Doctors are now able to use tools with optical fibers. **Optical fibers** are very thin tubes that allow light to pass through them. Doctors use cameras with optical fibers to see inside the body. A doctor can also perform keyhole surgery. This means that the doctor only makes a small cut. This way, the patient may have less pain and heal faster.

People make machines to do things they would not be able to do in other ways. X-rays let doctors see inside our bodies and can be used to find a cavity. It can also be used to find a broken bone. X-ray can even be used to treat cancer. But too much X-ray contact can lead to burns or cancer. Nuclear magnetic resonance (NMR) technology lets doctors see things that do not show up on X-rays such as what is happening inside blood vessels.

© Pearson Education, Inc. 4

Quick Study

Lesson 1 Checkpoint

1. What trouble has some technology caused in the United States and other countries?

_____

_____

2. How did an item found in nature play a role in the invention of Velcro™?

_____

_____

3. **Main Idea and Details** Which details support the main idea that in-line skating gear is made from many different materials?

_____

_____

_____

4. How do doctors use new medical technology in surgeries?

_____

_____

5. Compare and contrast the benefits of X-rays with the harmful qualities.

_____

_____

_____

Lesson 2: How has technology changed communication and transportation?

Vocabulary

communication the process of sending any type of message from one place to another

telecommunications communications that are done electronically

vehicle something that carries people and goods from one place to another; includes cars, trucks, trains, ships, planes, and rockets

Communication

Can you remember the last time you talked on the phone or sent an e-mail message? These are ways of communicating. **Communication** is the process of sending a message from one place to another. You can communicate in many ways. For example, you may use speech or writing.

Good communication has three parts. First, you must send a message. Second, the message must be received. Third, the message must be understood.

Can you think of some ways to send a message? Long ago, speech was the only way to send a message. But messages could not travel far. The message may not have been remembered. Then writing was invented. Messages could be sent long distances. Messages could be stored for a long time.

Telecommunications

Life changed when electricity was used for communication. Messages traveled faster. People all over the world could communicate with each other.

Today we communicate using telephones, radios, and televisions. These are kinds of telecommunications. **Telecommunications** are communications that are done electronically. A transmitter sends out a signal with information. The signal travels to a receiver. The receiver turns that signal back into a clear message. Telecommunications allow people to communicate with each other quickly.

Transportation Systems

Transportation systems move people and goods from place to place. Most modern transportation systems use a vehicle. A **vehicle** carries people and goods. Cars, trucks, ships, planes, trains, and rockets are vehicles. Vehicles move on roads, railways, waterways, and through airways. To make vehicles safer, for example, seat belts, air bags, and bumpers have been designed for cars.

Today, transportation systems often use computer technology. Computers keep these systems working properly.

The Technology of Time Measurement

Keeping track of time has always been important to us. Astronomers in ancient Egypt used the Sun's movement to tell time. Today we use clocks and watches. These measurements are more accurate than using the Sun.

Name _____

Lesson 2 Checkpoint

1. In what ways did life change when electricity was used with communication?

_____

_____

_____

2. How does the way we measure time today different from the way the ancient Egyptians measured it?

_____

_____

_____

3. **Main Idea and Details** What are some details that support the main idea that most modern transportation systems use vehicles?

_____

_____

_____